AMERICAN VALUES

CONTRIBUTIONS IN AMERICAN STUDIES

Series Editor: Robert H. Walker

American Values

Continuity and Change

Ralph H. *Henry* Gabriel

With an Introduction by Robert H. Walker

CONTRIBUTIONS IN AMERICAN STUDIES
NUMBER 15

GREENWOOD PRESS

Westport, Connecticut • London, England

Library of Congress Cataloging in Publication Data

Gabriel, Ralph Henry, 1890-
    American values; continuity and change.

    (Contributions in American studies, no. 15)
    Bibliography: p.
    1. United States—Civilization—Collected works.
I. Title.
E169.1.G22   917.3'03   74-24
ISBN 0-8371-7355-8

Library of Congress Catalog Card Number: 74-24
ISBN: 0-8371-7355-8

First published in 1974

Greenwood Press, a division of Williamhouse-Regency Inc.
51 Riverside Avenue, Westport, Connecticut 06880

Manufactured in the United States of America

To the Memory of David M. Potter

Contents

vii

Editor's Introduction

The most important thing about these essays as a collected body of work is the way they extend one of the most important theses about the meaning of the American national experience. While some scholars were still debating the legitimacy of the concept of national character, and while others were worrying about the question of investigative methods in a new field called American studies, Ralph Henry Gabriel went quietly and diligently to work. He showed how a continuum in the American faith could be demonstrated and how this continuum explained the events and ideas it underlay.

These essays were brought together at the suggestion of the series editor.* They were selected from a long list of possibilities and may seem, at first glance, more miscellaneous than cohesive. They were written or appeared between 1938 and 1964. Their titles

---

*Ralph Gabriel has seen this essay and has been kind enough to correct factual errors; he has, in the process, blue-penciled all of my large claims for the eminence of his work. On this subject I have invoked my scholar's right to disagree and my editor's right to the last word, *stet*. Although I am a biased witness, I suspect time is already on my side in the matter of these judgments.

reveal a broad range of pertinence to the American experience: Jefferson and the Enlightenment, religion and traditional values, romanticism and the spirit of history, constitutional democracy and the Cold War. They vary also in form: some were addresses, some pamphlets, some periodical articles. Each stands by itself, carrying a complete set of thoughts and observations related to a specific theme or subject. Yet they also share an important common thread.

This common thread traces many figures and patterns, but raised in the midst of these embroideries are the two editions, published in 1940 and 1956, of Ralph Gabriel's *magnum opus, The Course of American Democratic Thought*. As this book enunciates one of the major interpretive statements about America, so the essays in the present collection reveal its genesis, document its testings and applications, and show a scholar placing his theory of history up against the major events of his own lifetime. The opening essay, "Constitutional Democracy: A Nineteenth-Century Faith," was, the author says flatly, "the beginning of *The Course of American Democratic Thought*."

In this book, Thomas Mann's definition of history as that which has happened and goes on happening in time sounded the keynote. Notably among scholars, Ralph Gabriel has been unwilling to stop with a theory that explained the remote past. These essays are particularly impressive for their application of historical wisdom to such modern turning points as the fall of France, the coming of World War II, the atom bomb, the Cold War and after. *The Course of American Democratic Thought* illustrated mainly the first half of Mann's definition; these essays help fulfill the second half while they reveal further roots and relevance in the past. The close relationship between that book and these essays makes it impossible to discuss one without the other.

When *The Course of American Democratic Thought* appeared, its author had been a full professor at Yale for twelve years. He had published enough books and articles to fill several academic lifetimes, but very little that would obviously prefigure the work that was printed in his fiftieth year. Yet there was a clear kind of preparation which the discerning reader of Professor Gabriel's bibliography will perceive: an intellectual initiation founded on the very rocks and soil of the continent, proceeding through an interest in the aborigines, the backgrounds of the European Enlightenment, and the experience of the Revolutionary generation. Very early there was a groping for perimeters: land and sea, Indians and settlers, politicians and preachers, men of war and men of peace. In fact, judging from the published evidence, Ralph Gabriel's comprehension of America was so extensive that only a work of uncompromising synthesis would serve to bring it to fulfillment.

With unusual unanimity, the book review editors of the academic journals sensed the importance of *The Course of American Democratic Thought* and assigned appropriate talents to greet it. Among those who accepted this assignment in 1940 were Harry Elmer Barnes, Charles A. Beard, Crane Brinton, Henry S. Commager, Howard M. Jones, Roy F. Nichols, and T. V. Smith. To a man they treated it as a major work: not a continuation of Parrington, wrote Professor Commager, who later took up this task himself, but a work that decidedly ranked with Parrington. All of them would surely have agreed with another reviewer (L. L. Bernard, in *The American Sociology Review* 6 [April 1941]: 302) that many "less able works have been awarded Pulitzer prizes." Beyond accord as to its weight, the reviewers offered no easy consensus. Several of them commended the author for avoiding the pitfall of identifying ideas with actions. Most of them praised his broad and subjective use of source materials. Many of them found the method exciting and original.

Yet, with the benefit of another edition and thirty years of hindsight, it would seem that few of these eminent reviewers penetrated to the core of the book as well as Crane Brinton—the only historian among them whose specialty was *not* the United States. While most comments on the two chapters dealing with

symbolism were puzzled or unfavorable, Professor Brinton sin-
gled them out as worthy of elaboration into a whole book devoted
to "the place of such symbolism in the development of our society." (*The Yale Law Journal* 50 [December 1940]: 360.) He then
described it as "a history of the *values* [italics his] these men
cherished—primarily, therefore, a history of ethical and political
ideas—but so widely taken as to draw on almost every field with
which the American mind has concerned itself." (359) If *The
Course of American Democratic Thought* is most importantly to be
viewed as a history of American values, then the essays in this
collection take on the added burden of showing how many of them
were derived, and—once derived—how they were applied to
American situations past and contemporary.

The allusions to Commager, Bernard, and Brinton suggest that,
even though consensus did not truly exist among the critics of
Ralph Gabriel's book, there were certain recurring comments.
Indeed, some qualities were noted with sufficient frequency as to
suggest themselves as a theme for this introductory essay. They
can be made, usefully and constructively, to summarize the most
important contributions of this author in his professional life. With
only slight extensions, they also depict the man. They are the
qualities of scope, originality, and unity.

The wide familiarity which enabled Ralph Gabriel "to draw on
almost every field with which the American mind has concerned
itself" began with an undergraduate concentration on geology and
geography, an interest that continued through the publication of
his first titles. As a graduate student and young faculty member at
Yale, he cultivated a close association with sociologists and an-
thropologists at a time when the latter were formulating the concept of culture and were undertaking the description and analysis
of this phenomenon of collective human life. Growing up in rural
upstate New York gave him a familiarity with farming which
—added to his academic knowledge of the American land—made
it natural for him to write of the farmer in the Commonwealth and

of toilers on the land. Familiarity with place also made him a devotee of local history, a skill he has applied not only to Long Island and other parts of New York, but also to New England and the West. Approaching the study of the West in 1929, he subtitled one of his *Pageant of America* volumes "A Story of Race Relations." Twelve years later he was to publish his study of that unusual Cherokee, Elias Boudinot. He understood the importance of relations not only between red and white but also between black and white, as he showed particularly in the eighth essay in the present collection, "The Cold War and Changes in American Thought."

Ralph Gabriel's interest in early America produced valuable pieces on St. Jean de Crèvecoeur, Ezra Stiles, Timothy Dwight, and Thomas Jefferson, on the Revolutionary generation and their European intellectual heritage. Other works dealt with the Civil War, the role and image of the military in American life, the consequences of twentieth-century wars, and even the impact of military government. Admiring the pen at least as much as the sword, he used the best of American literature to make his historical points. To the *Literary History of the United States* he contributed a thorough and perceptive chapter on Mark Twain. The thoughts of scientists and the achievements of inventors from the early tinkerers of New Haven to the developers of cybernetics and the H-bomb have also come within his large scope.

While many of his contemporaries were accepting Marxism or some other form of determinism, Professor Gabriel kept insisting on the vital place of religion in national and institutional life. Philosophy, ethics, morality—the most humane and exalted aspects of humanism are unavoidably present in his work, explicitly in some, implicitly in all. Such scope, accompanied by a high level of competence and an omnipresent sense of quality, has produced a master of generalizations, an author of texts, an appraiser of the deepest cultural values.

Another kind of scope may also be observed in Professor

Gabriel's unusual dedication to the art of teaching. Before entering Yale, he had been initiated as a teacher in the two-room schoolhouse of a rural hamlet, thus opening a career that has continued almost without recess for over sixty years. As recently as 1971 he brought out the latest in a long and highly successful series of junior high school history texts. One of the most interesting essays on the changing values of the twentieth century he wrote for an audience of secondary school social studies teachers. It was he, more than any other single person, who broke the new ground in theory and method that made Yale's *Chronicles of America* series the effective teaching device it became. The lessons learned in preparing manuals, editorial apparatus, and theoretical defenses for this general history course bore fruit in the enormously popular undergraduate course Professor Gabriel taught at Yale both individually and with the late Stanley T. Williams.

Wherever he went he taught. His work with the *Chronicles* extended to home study. In the autumn of 1941, at the request of General Ben Lear, he wrote for the Second Army a series of lectures on American topics which were later published for classroom use. His commitment to UNESCO produced a most useful introduction to American values for foreigners. His sallies abroad—to Cambridge, Salzburg, Kyoto, Tokyo, Sydney—have left a series of warm and special lessons about the culture he brought with him.

At home his students have described his seminars to be more evocative than any educational experience in their lives. These classes in the graduate school at Yale have produced a series of able professors who have mirrored the Gabriel seminars from San Francisco to Williamstown. And to many who have never had the joy of sitting formally before this highly versatile and professional teacher, there has been a mountain of shared wisdom unpretentiously given and gratefully accepted.

In outlining the scope of this teacher-scholar's achievements, it has been impossible to ignore some areas of originality. Some of these contributions can be alluded to with great brevity. But the individual familiar with pedagogy and scholarship in American history over the last fifty years will want to give each of them a moment's respectful consideration.

Many younger scholars and teachers have acted as though they were discovering materials and techniques never used or imagined before. For example, following on the heels of the "new math" and "new physics" in the mid-1960s came another version of "the new history." This time the stress was on teaching through documents contemporary to the period under study. Textbooks were eschewed and students were encouraged to react directly to the original materials. As early as 1937, however, Ralph Gabriel —with Harry R. Warfel and Stanley T. Williams—had published a collection of source materials designed for exactly this purpose.

Another seemingly modern development favors the use of visual materials as a strong complement to the printed word. No one has said that picture books are something new; nor has it been rare for writers of history to illustrate their texts with photographs and drawings. But *The Pageant of America*, as defined by Ralph Gabriel in 1925, was something else again. It was and remains a remarkable collaboration between the visual record and the written comment. In this 15-volume series, words and images work together at a creative level that was not achieved again until decades later. It anticipated many topics (such as the serious history of sport and entertainment) which are today being "discovered" under the heading of popular culture. The organization of this series gives further room to appreciate the prescience of its editor. It reflects the realization that American history needed study not just by period or even by region, but that there were also special topics and groups (workers, farmers, Indians, fishermen) which needed their own sustained attention. In the attitudes he fostered toward many of these groups, Ralph Gabriel seems very contemporary—a remarkable feat for someone writing and working before the Great Depression and the shifts in attitude which accompanied it.

Ralph Gabriel entered the history department at Yale at a time when "social history" was a relatively new concept. Debates were still raging over what this newly identified branch of historical writing was to be and become. In spite of many fine arguments to the contrary, social history still suffered from the charge of amorphousness. Social history, critics derided, was nothing but what was left when political, military, and diplomatic history had been removed. And, of course, there was some truth in the allegation. It was also true that persuasive efforts to find a central focus or an organizing principle in social history were rare indeed. Surely one of the most important, and in many ways original, contributions of social historian Gabriel was to illustrate one way of giving depth and meaning to that discipline: through a concentration on prevailing ideas and values.

To the emerging approach to knowledge called American studies Ralph Gabriel also gave an important and original stamp. His presence was crucial in developing what for years has been the largest and most effective undergraduate major in American studies and in creating a graduate program which has produced an overwhelming number of its leading teachers and scholars. Among the important American studies programs significantly shaped by Yale alumni are those at San Francisco State, Denver, Texas, Stetson, Emory, Brown, and Pennsylvania. Professor Gabriel helped make this field of study a primarily humanistic one, where literature, philosophy, religion, and the arts took a major place. The history of ideas and intellectual history, two subtly but importantly different disciplines, took their meaning against this background. But the role of Ralph Gabriel, grounded as he was in the physical and social sciences, was to preserve an academic climate where methods and materials from nonhumanistic disciplines could play a part as well. The American studies program at

Yale has been carefully nurtured; it has made a spectacle of itself in no way but through its sound, continuing, and growing success. His colleagues freely acknowledge that no one has been as important in this process, from the beginning, as Ralph Gabriel.

Ralph Gabriel's greatest stroke of originality, however, lies in the method which produced *The Course of American Democratic Thought* and the essays collected in this volume. It is a method so unostentatious as to have escaped even those eminent reviewers of 1940. On the surface that book and these essays are indeed a history of the influential ideas held by representative or influential Americans since 1815. What unifies these ideas? The tenets of the American democratic faith. In identifying and arranging these tenets, the author developed a method so unusual as to remind one at times more of psychoanalysis than of conventional history. How does one discover the root values of a culture? By observing it in times of crisis. Torn in two directions, the nation will be petitioned by opposed leaders in opposing directions. To what basic convictions will these leaders appeal? Some arguments will vary with time and place, but some will remain constant. Those arguments—the ones used by both sides in vital national debates—identify the basic beliefs and values held by the culture. So ran the substratum of logic beneath the persuasive essays that make up much of this collection and all of *The Course of American Democratic Thought*.

A good, if microcosmic, piece of historiographical research will be done some day on the reasons behind the simplification of the American democratic faith from four tenets in 1940 to three in 1956. Was it just that the author asked himself the question "progress toward what?" and concluded that since progress only defined commitment to the other three tenets—the worth of the free individual, the existence of a fundamental law and the special mission of America—that it could logically be dropped? The author once agreed to my statement of this case to him, but he is an agreeable man, and I think the question might have been more complex than he cared to entertain at that moment. Having centered some of my own reading lately on the related questions of growth, progress, and expansion, I am struck by the fact that Professor Gabriel chose to open his coverage of the democratic faith at just that moment when a new, dynamic, nonlinear concept of progress was entering the culture. I am likewise impressed that, long before other scholars or public figures, he seems to have sensed that "progress" was no longer to be an unqualified American goal. Articles on this subject have shown a faith in progress lasting well into the 1960s and beyond. Yet, sometime between 1940 and 1956, Professor Gabriel saw that progress was too unshaded a term or too special a phenomenon to characterize American culture with consistent accuracy from 1815 to the moving present. The best clue to his reasons may well lie in the present volume.

The values discovered in *The Course of American Democratic Thought* and these essays are different from those listed by a scholar who is more purely a social scientist, like Robin Williams, or a scholar who is more purely an historian, like Arthur M. Schlesinger. As one compares these other lists with that of Professor Gabriel, particularly in this time of shifting cultural values, one may be forced to conclude that whereas Ralph Gabriel's list is shorter and less descriptive, it represents a phenomenal effort to identify those values which are least subject to the shifts in philosophical fashion and the vagaries of cultural change.

The exemplification of scope and originality could extend almost indefinitely; the recognition of unifying forces must, by definition, be much more succinct. Three such forces have been important in the career of Ralph Gabriel: an institution, a field of learning, and a concept. When Yale College opened its doors to a young man from Watkins Glen, there began an association which continues to this day and which has produced considerable good on both sides. Ralph Gabriel earned three degrees there. Near the end of his career as a graduate student and instructor, he joined the army and served for more than a year, after which, as he puts it, "we went home to Yale."

Yale, with its great library, its excellent students, its active press, and its diverse and stimulating faculty, has been a good place for Ralph Gabriel. Much of what Yale has to give is evident in his work. The relationship, however, has been anything but onesided. Among Ralph Gabriel's first professional efforts was the task of making Yale's extensive *Chronicles of America* series an effective teaching collection in several contexts. What he has done for and with the Yale University Press would itself fill a career. He has also written an important segment of Yale's history and served long on the board of Yale-in-China.

At the end of World War I, the history department at Yale welcomed back the discharged lieutenant with his fresh doctorate of philosophy and soon made him an assistant professor. He was promoted crisply through the academic ranks and became the holder of an endowed chair which he now occupies *emeritus*. Letting rest the question of the deep, human, and personal returns Ralph Gabriel has made to Yale, it could fairly be said that in the last fifty years very few students have passed through Yale in the fields of history, American studies, or the humanities without having been exposed, directly or indirectly, to the many contributions that have marked the career of Ralph Gabriel at Yale.

The way in which one institution has served as a focus for many of Ralph Gabriel's professional activities is paralleled by the way in which the discipline of history has centered the ideas of his broadly ranging mind. To the subject matter of history he brought the unfamiliar materials of geography, local studies, religion and biography. He arranged them in a number of ways: in texts; in pictures and film strips; as monographs, special studies, articles, and reviews. To the teaching of history he gave special thought, for his student audience ranged from soldiers and extension readers to graduate scholars. To the concept of history he gave all the rigor of careful analysis of the past along with a disproportionate insistence on history as a continuing force in perceiving the present and the future.

Ralph Gabriel's career as a historian has been unified by one particular concept: a search for human values. To appreciate what this search has meant to him one must probably begin by recognizing his relatively elevated vision of the human condition. To Ralph Gabriel individuals and groups are capable of transcending the determinism of physical conditions or social forces. The religious experience is a real one. Fundamental moral laws can be recognized by individuals and by groups, a recognition that sometimes affects history as much as drought, depression, or violence. The case may be put even more strongly, for there is an implicit assumption in the canon of this historian that places the greatest worth on that historical activity which helps men and women recognize their deeper ethical and moral roots and equips them to apply this tradition to an understanding of the past and an accommodation to the present. Whether this morality springs from nature or God, whether it works through church or congress, whether it be judged by individual or collective criteria, it is the unique essential of the human life. Thus, American values are not only very particular but are also very importantly universal, human values.

Colleagues who have never met Ralph Gabriel are often as enthusiastic about his work as those of us who have been fortunate enough to know him. Such is the benign force of his unaffected personality that, having known him, it is impossible to consider oneself impartial again. The point of the foregoing paragraphs has been to place the collected essays in as constructive an interpretive light as possible. If "constructive" has become "adulatory," I apologize. I think my appreciation of the work of this man is genuinely professional, but it could not help being colored by a personal fondness and admiration. Fortunately, there are many who will read these pages and share this happy confusion between respect for the man and esteem for the work.

Ralph Henry Gabriel was born on April 29, 1890, in Reading,

New York, and was raised near the quiet rural town of Watkins Glen which, eventually, became associated with the noisy modern sport of automobile racing. Since the fall of 1909, when he matriculated at Yale, his home has been New Haven, except for a few years following his retirement when he accepted an invitation to establish an American studies program for American University's new School of International Service. There he went in 1958, taught until 1963 when he became a professor *emeritus* for the second time, lingered a while in Washington, writing and preparing his Phi Beta Kappa lectures, and then returned to New Haven. I have shared many days with him at the Library of Congress, admiring his compact, effective work day, and standing in awe of his daily achievements. But I know he was glad, as a researcher, to return to the familiarity of the Yale library.

In addition to his active service in World War I, he responded to the call during World War II by moving to Charlottesville, Virginia, and helping to staff the War Department School of Military Government. Immediately after the wars, he accepted a visitor's chair at the University of Sydney where, as a recent visit of my own can testify, he is strongly and warmly remembered. In 1964 he lectured under Fulbright-Hays provisions at the University of Tokyo and that summer organized, as senior visitor, the Kyoto Seminar in American Studies. In 1951-1952 he was Pitt Professor at Cambridge University, which institution awarded him an honorary degree, as have also Bucknell, Colgate, and Williams. In 1961-1963 he was president of the American Studies Association.

An important chapter in the nonprofessional life of Ralph Gabriel began when he was still a very young man earning money for his education by teaching in the village school. Concerned that one of his young students had been long absent from class, he paid a visit to her home and found her suffering from an attenuated illness. During the long period in which her doctor-father prescribed no exertion—not even that of conversation with a visitor—the young teacher, bringing his guitar, came on occasion to lighten the tedium of the sick room with a few songs. The student, Christine Davis, eventually recovered and, by a less mysterious process, became Mrs. Gabriel a decade later. In their many years at New Haven, Christine Gabriel bore and reared their three children. According to a legion of younger faculty and graduate students, it was "Chrissie and Ralph" who successfully bridged the gap between generations in the Yale history department. The flyleaf of Ralph Gabriel's major work reads, "This book is for C.D.G."

A many-generationed view of the Gabriels is in their summer setting on a handsome New England lake. There, many years ago, they purchased a lodge and surrounding land from what had once been a tutoring camp. The lodge is gracious and inviting with its rustic porch part open and part enclosed, facing the still cove and the adjoining lake. Behind the lodge is a flat clearing where, when children and grandchildren come to visit, a sleeping tent has been pitched. A few yards away is a small cabin where the elder Gabriels sleep, leaving the lakefront lodge, its pier and boats, to the younger guests. Still farther from the water, in a woods of pine and birch, is a still smaller cabin—just big enough for a man, a desk, a few bookshelves, and a typewriter. The entire establishment carries the name its first owners soon after the turn of the century gave it, "Aloha"; never was so appropriate a word so accidentally applied.

The unity that characterizes Ralph Gabriel's intellectual life translates readily into such personal qualities as loyalty and steadfastness. In addition, this man has a plainness of manner and a lack of pretentiousness—disarming qualities in one who has earned the right to considerable deference. And there are the continuing curiosity, the largeness of concept, the warmth of humanity, and the instinct to be helpful in the largest possible way. As one who has admired his personal as well as professional achievements, I would like to close by applying to both the man and his work the resounding old-fashioned tribute with which Charles A. Beard closed his review (*The American Historical Review* 46 [October 1940]: 165): "Let him who thinks that he can draw the arrow to the head take up Mr. Gabriel's bow and test his strength and skill."

Robert H. Walker, Series Editor
May 1973
Washington, D. C.

PART ONE

The essays in this part reflect reactions to contemporary events and develop an interpretive thesis relating to national values.

1

Constitutional Democracy: A Nineteenth-Century Faith

The group of anxious men who assembled at Philadelphia in 1787 to frame a constitution for the new United States had almost universally that confidence in human reason which stemmed from Newton's scientific achievements of the century before, and back of that from the triumphs of the classical philosophers. Americans were interested in the individual man. Democracy is the appropriate political expression of the atomistic social emphasis, yet many of the framers had a healthy skepticism of democracy. To some it suggested the triumph of mediocrity, and to others the substitution of the rule of passion for that of reason. But the United States was committed to the principle of democracy by the logic of the Revolution, and, as a consequence, the framers established their government in frank Lockean style upon the consent of the governed. In the framing of their great document they were both

SOURCE: Reprinted with permission of Columbia University Press, from *The Constitution Reconsidered*, ed. Conyers Read (New York, 1938), p. 247-258. Copyright 1938 by Columbia University Press.

3

rationalists and empiricists. When they were done, they rightly looked upon themselves as initiating a great experiment in popular government.

Fifty years passed. When Americans of the new generation met to celebrate the fiftieth anniversary of their constitution, they remarked that the experimental period had passed. The demonstration of the efficacy of popular sovereignty had been made. Under it the United States had become an important nation. The fears of the fathers concerning democracy had not been justified by later events, and with Andrew Jackson the common man, now skilled in the political art, had come to power.

Americans of the middle period lived in a climate of opinion different from that of the Founding Fathers. Eighteenth-century Deism, charged with causing the excesses of the French Revolution, had long since been driven underground. Tom Paine, returning as an old man to America, had found the doors of respectability closed and had gone to a lonely death. Evangelical Protestantism was covering the nation like a rising tide and reached its apogee in the middle decade of the nineteenth century. The popular symbol of social stability for this generation was not, as in our day, the Constitution of the United States or the Supreme Court, but was rather the village church, whose spire pointed significantly heavenward. "Civilization," remarked Emerson, "depends on morality." And it was the almost universal belief of his generation that morality rests upon religion. But Emerson was disgusted with the anthropomorphism of the conventional Christianity of his day and was dissatisfied with the pale negations of Unitarianism. He announced his transcendentalism in a little book entitled *Nature*, published in 1836, the year before the fiftieth anniversary of the Constitution. Four years later, an inconspicuous citizen named George Sidney Camp wrote a small volume which he called *Democracy*, and which Harper and Brothers thought expressed so well the mood of the age that they published it in their Family Library and later brought out a second edition. "Faith," said

Camp, "is as necessary to the republican as to the Christian, and the fundamental characteristic of both."[1] "We are born believing," added Emerson. "A man bears beliefs as a tree bears apples."[2] Faith is the clue to understanding the democracy of the middle period.

Among these Americans the word "democracy" took on two different but interrelated connotations; it had both a realistic and a romantic meaning. Realistic democracy was a behavior pattern which included caucuses and logrolling, the struggle for office among individuals, and the sparring for advantage among sections or pressure groups. Romantic democracy was a cluster of ideas which made up a national faith and which, though unrecognized as such, had the power of a state religion. Some of these ideas were as old as classical Greece and others were as new as the American nation. But, though most of the ideas were old and were borrowed, the configuration of the cluster was unique.

A secular national religion, such as the communism of Lenin's Russia or the national socialism of contemporary Germany, must meet certain basic psychological needs of the people who profess it. Among a disunited people it must emphasize the group and its solidarity. To a depressed people or to one suffering from a sense of inferiority it must give that illusion of superiority which springs from the doctrine that the nation has a great mission to perform in the world. To an anxious people, fearful of the future, a national religion must give a sense of security. In the America of the middle period, unity was a primary problem. Those transportation facilities which bind a nation together could not keep pace with the rapid westward advance of the frontier. Climatic differences had created a social problem which threatened the United States with division along sectional lines. The United States faced the menace of separatism. A lesser mid-nineteenth-century American need was for some defense against a sense of inferiority to Europe. This became acute in the middle period because in that age Americans were sensing their intellectual and their national power at a time when foreign travelers, some of them of the prominence of Dickens, were coming in increasing numbers and were returning to the Old World to write frequently unjust and almost universally offensive books. In such a scene Ralph Waldo Emerson threw off the robes of a Unitarian clergyman. He announced in 1836 the cosmic philosophy upon which his transcendentalism was founded. He proclaimed in 1837 in his famous Phi Beta Kappa address at Harvard College the American declaration of intellectual independence. "We have listened too long to the courtly muses of Europe," he said to the young scholars before him. "We will walk on our own feet; we will work with our own hands; we will speak our own minds."[3] From that day Emerson became the Isaiah of that democratic faith which was at that very moment taking form spontaneously among the American people.

The foundation of this democratic faith was a frank supernaturalism derived from Christianity. The twentieth-century student is often astonished at the extent to which supernaturalism permeated American thought of the nineteenth century. The basic postulate of the democratic faith affirmed that God, the creator of man, has also created a moral law for his government and has endowed him with a conscience with which to apprehend it. Underneath and supporting human society, as the basic rock supports the hills, is a moral order which is the abiding place of the eternal principles of truth and righteousness. The reiteration of this doctrine of the moral order runs through mid-nineteenth-century social and political thought like the rhythm of the drums through the forest scene of O'Neill's *Emperor Jones.* "There are principles of abstract justice which the creator of all things has impressed on the mind of his creature man," said John Marshall in 1823 in an opinion from the bench, "and which are admitted to regulate, in a great degree, the rights of civilized nations."[4] "In ascending to the great principles upon which all society rests," added Justice Joseph Story in 1828, "it must be admitted that there are some which are of eternal obligation, and arise from our common dependence upon our Creator. Among these are the duty to do justice, to love mercy, and to walk humbly before God."[5] "There is a higher law," proclaimed William Ellery Channing long before Seward's famous speech in the Senate, "even Virtue, Rectitude, the Voice of Conscience, the Will of God."[6] "The moral law," said Emerson in 1836, "lies at the center of nature and radiates to the circumference."[7]

To trace the origin or the history of this doctrine of a higher or fundamental law is not our present task, for to do so would be to examine one of the more important strands of thought in Western civilization. Suffice it to say that in the United States in the middle years of the nineteenth century the existence of a moral order which was not the creation of man but which served as the final guide for his behavior was almost universally assumed among thinking persons. For Christians the moral law was the will of God; for the small company of articulate free thinkers it was the natural law of eighteenth-century Deism. Mr. Justice Story in his *Commentaries on the Constitution* succeeded in phrasing the doctrine in terms which would be acceptable both to those who still found their guide in reason and to those who looked for direction to the Scriptures. "The rights of conscience," said he, "are given by God, and cannot be encroached upon by human authority, without criminal disobedience of the precepts of natural, as well as of revealed, religion."[8] Before the moral law all men stood on a footing of equality; from it they derived equal rights. Among the latter was the right to the private ownership of property.

The universal acceptance of the doctrine of the moral order suggests that it had uses in the culture of the time. American skies were darkened during the middle period by a storm which gathered momentum and increased in intensity with the passing years. The controversy over human slavery put the realistic democracy of American political institutions to the test of the hurricane. Anger mounted on either side, and, long before the final break occurred, passion threatened to replace reason in the councils of the nation.

Garrison in the North and Yancey in the South early advocated breaking the ties which bound the sections together. Americans turned to the Constitution as the fundamental law of the land for those common agreements between the contending parties without which debate is impossible. But this instrument appeared to fail them. Instead of resolving the dispute, the Constitution became the very center of controversy as the sections divided on the question of its origin and of its nature. Webster for the North affirmed that the document drawn up at Philadelphia was the supreme law for a nation; Calhoun for the South replied that it was no more than a compact among sovereign states. The positions were at opposite poles and were irreconcilable; yet faith in constitutionalism was not shaken. Even after the final break the Confederacy did not abandon constitutionalism. The event suggests that the American faith in constitutional democracy did not have its ultimate origin in the constitution which established it. Emerson in 1854 sought to explain the paradox. "Whenever a man," said he, "has come to this state of mind, that there is no church for him but his believing prayer, no Constitution but his dealing well and justly with his neighbor; no liberty but his invincible will to do right, then certain aids and allies will promptly appear; for the constitution of the Universe is on his side."[9] The doctrine of the moral order was, in effect, a doctrine of cosmic constitutionalism. The body of natural and of moral law was the fixed and unchangeable constitution of the world. The fundamental law of the Republic was thought to be but a man-made imitation of a divine archetype. When it failed to provide those common agreements necessary to rational debate, recourse must be had to those unwritten and eternal principles which, in the universal belief of Americans, made society possible. Emerson, in appealing to the "constitution of the Universe," was discussing the Fugitive Slave Law to which he was opposed. Southern proponents of the peculiar institution, despairing of the Federal Constitution, were at the same time founding their defense of slavery upon the same moral law. "Negroes are not free," said

George Fitzhugh, "because God and nature, and the general good, and their own good, intended them for slaves."[10] The doctrine of the moral order was here providing those agreements which by functioning as the foundation of logical discussion made it possible for the democratic process to continue. Because Americans believed that fixed laws and eternal principles underlay society, they believed in written constitutions. But these, after all, were experiments, as the delegates at Philadelphia had suggested. If constitutions should fail, as the Federal Constitution failed in 1861, they should be reconstructed, as the Confederates tried to do, in accordance with unfolding human experience and with new light on the nature of the moral order.

The arguments of Emerson and of Fitzhugh sound strange in our post-Versailles world in which the prestige of Christianity has declined and naturalistic philosophies have captured the social disciplines. The absolutism of the nineteenth century which expressed itself in the theory of the moral law is out of fashion in our America. Faith in the eternal character of right and wrong is in retreat before the advance of the pragmatic ethics of expediency. But the retreat has not yet ended and, while it continues, modern Americans are confused. The bitter fruit of their confusion is a sense of intellectual and of social insecurity. Our age is witnessing many attempts of individuals and of groups to escape from the malaise of insecurity, but nothing in America is more pathetic or, perhaps, more menacing than the efforts of those who would set up the Constitution as a fetish and worship it in the spirit of the tribe which prays to idols of its own making. There was no Constitution-worship before Sumter fell. The Webster-Calhoun debate prevented it and the doctrine of the moral order made it unnecessary. That article of faith gave to mid-nineteenth-century Americans that mental peace and that sense of security which comes to the man who feels that he has planted his feet upon the eternal rock.

The second doctrine of the democratic faith of the middle period was that of the free individual. It contained a theory of liberty and of the relation of the individual to the state which he ultimately governed. The doctrine was derived from that of the moral order. The path which led from the one to the other was a philosophy of progress. This philosophy affirmed that the advance of civilization is measured by the progress of men in apprehending and in translating into individual and social action the eternal principles which comprise the moral law. The advance of civilization, in other words, is the progress of virtue. "Nothing can be plainer," remarked William C. Jarvis, counselor at law, in 1820, "than that the barbarian in the desert requires the restraint of a more powerful arm than the individuals whose passions and propensities are under the eternal restraint of moral and religious sentiments."[11] "Civilization," added Frederick Grimke quaintly some thirty-six years later, "is that state in which the higher part of our nature is made to predominate over the lower."[12] Out of this concept that the civilized man is the virtuous man and this hopeful philosophy that mankind is on the march toward a better world came the nineteenth-century theory of liberty. As men become more nearly perfect in obedience to the fundamental moral law, as they develop what Irving Babbitt used to call the "inner check," they need less the external control of man-made laws. "Hence," insisted Emerson, following Jefferson, "the less government the better. . . . The antidote to the abuse of formal government is the growth of influence of private character, the growth of the Individual. . . . To educate the wise man the State exists, and with the appearance of the wise man the State expires."[13]

Henry Thoreau, Emerson's Concord friend, carried this reasoning to its logical conclusion. The man who has achieved moral maturity, he thought, should reject imperfect laws made by stupid majorities and should accept the higher law which is disclosed by his conscience as the sole guide and regulator of his life. In particular, he should practice civil disobedience when the state embarks upon an immoral policy. The fiery Thoreau emphasized his point by going to jail rather than pay a Massachusetts poll tax which he assumed would be spent to further iniquitous policies. That such extremism was rare in nineteenth-century America, however, was illustrated by Emerson's anxious visit to his friend behind the bars. "Henry," asked the great transcendentalist, "why are you here?" "Waldo," replied the jailbird, "why are you not here?" Emerson, the hardheaded Yankee farmer, thought such extremism in the nineteenth century would defeat its own ends. "We think our civilization is near its meridian," Emerson remarked, "but we are only yet at the cock-crowing and the morning star. In our barbarous society the influence of character is in its infancy." [14] But before Emerson, as before Thoreau, shone the ideal of liberty as the ultimate goal, of liberty not as a means to an end but as an end in itself. "Liberty," said Emerson, "is an accurate index, in men and nations, of general progress." [15] He was the greatest of the preachers of the democratic faith. He traveled from end to end of America preaching his gospel of self-reliant individualism. He moved the young men of the middle period as no other figure of the age. He opened doors for them which enabled them to escape from the stuffy confines of evangelical Protestantism into a glorious out-of-doors. He filled the disciples of the democratic faith with the hope of a better and freer world in the creation of which they would have a share.

It has commonly been said that the exaltation of the individual and the apotheosis of liberty of the mid-nineteenth century was the natural result of certain economic and social factors. A relatively small population was scattered over a vast area. Capitalistic enterprise had not developed beyond the stage in which its most important figure was the individual entrepreneur. Inevitably in such a social scene the focus of attention must be upon the individual. The conquest of a wilderness in the West and the attempt to establish a new industrialism in the East put a premium upon individual initiative and hence on individual liberty. Important as were these factors, there was another of equal, if not greater, significance for the doctrine of liberty. Down to the very eve of the fall of Sumter,

Americans of the middle period enjoyed a sense of security rarely to be duplicated in modern history. Not only were there no dangerous potential enemies beyond the national frontiers holding the threat of invasion over the citizens of the Republic, but Americans marched in triumph into the capital of Mexico and dictated the terms of a profitable peace. An ocean guarded the eastern cities against attack from Europe. The opportunities of the frontier, moreover, offered to every able-bodied man the possibility of personal economic security. The doctrine of the moral law gave to the men of the middle period a sense of stability and of security in a world of change. The American philosophy of liberty had its seventeenth- and eighteenth-century origins in protests against established orders. It was then primarily a means to an end in itself, it rested squarely upon a universal sense of security. When the traditional foundations of a culture crumble, as we are seeing them do today and in the Western world crazed by nationalism, when government by law gives way to government by irresponsible force, the preoccupation with liberty as an end in itself is replaced by a new search for security, mental, social, economic, and even physical. In the middle period, however, when Americans felt safe, they could afford to enjoy their doctrine of the free individual.

The third doctrine of the democratic faith was that of the mission of America. It was a mid-nineteenth-century version of those myths of unique origin and of unique destiny so common in tribal tradition. Liberty, according to a widely accepted version of American mythology, had been established by deity in an empty Western continent so that, freed from the burden of European tradition, it might flourish and become an inspiration to the world.

> O God, beneath thy guiding hand
> Our exiled fathers crossed the sea . . .

sang Leonard Bacon in 1833.[16] George Bancroft, historian, saw the hand of the Omnipotent in the founding of the Republic. As late as 1866 Samuel Kirkland Lothrop, addressing a great Boston meeting upon the anniversary of the Declaration of Independence, proclaimed again the supernaturalistic interpretation of the origin of American democracy. "God in the hour of its utmost need," he declared, "gave . . . liberty an opportunity to plant itself on this new continent and strike its roots so deep that no despotic power could tear them up."[17] The doctrine of mission was merely an extension of that origin. "Standing where we now do," prophesied A. A. Bennet, addressing his neighbors of the New York frontier on the national anniversary of 1827, "we may look forward to the period when the spark kindled in America shall spread and spread, till the whole earth be illumined by its light."[18] "Already," added Justice Story in 1828, "has the age caught the spirit of our institutions."[19] Whitman distilled a folk belief into deathless verse.

Sail, sail thy best ship of Democracy
of Value is thy freight . . .
Thou holdst not the venture of thyself alone, nor of the Western
    continent alone . . .
With thee time voyages in trust, the antecedent nations sink or
    swim with thee,
Theirs, theirs as much as thine, the destination port triumphant.[20]

What was the significance of this doctrine of origin and of destiny? It provided the formula which expressed that sense of superiority that an in-group normally feels with respect to out-groups. It was the American way of saying: We are the Greeks; the rest of the world is made up of barbarians. As an expression of the American tribal ethnocentrism it assisted in that subtle osmosis by which a federation of particularist states was transformed into a united nation. But it did more even than strengthen and glorify the nation. It provided for American democracy, with its emphasis upon diversity, a philosophy of unity. And this doctrine of the destiny of America held up before the humble democrat, whose drab world rarely extended beyond the main street of his village, a romantic vision in which he could see his inconspicuous efforts after righteousness invested with a world significance.

If Emerson was the prophet and Whitman the poet of the democratic faith, Herman Melville, ex-whaler, was its savage critic. Putting his thought for the most part into allegory but permitting himself at times direct, barbed thrusts, he assailed every doctrine of the ruling creed of his age. How do you know, he asked the Christians in effect, that God has created a moral order? God is past finding out. To the most urgent questions of men God answers nothing. If religion offers no security, thought Melville, neither does science, for science is but a lightship whose rays illuminate a circle in the darkness. It is man's incomprehensible fate that his days are set in mystery and that the essence of his life is hazard. Melville thought that the fundamental delusion in his age was that absolutism which held both religion and science in an iron grip and which was the foundation of the democratic faith. Out of this absolutism came the doctrine of the moral law, the belief in progress, and the gospel of liberty as an end in itself. Phantasms all, thought Melville. Melville rejected eternals. Each age, he taught, is new. Each age has its good and its evil and to the end of time neither will conquer the other. He assailed in particular the belief in progress. ''There are many who erewhile believed that the age of pikes and javelins was passed,'' he said in *Mardi* in 1849, ''that after a heady and blustering youth . . . [the world] was at last settling down into a serene old age; and that the Indian summer, first discovered in your land [of America], sovereign kings! was the hazy vapour emitted from its tranquil pipe. But it has not so proved. The world's peaces are but truces. Long absent, at last the red comets have returned. And return they must, though their periods be ages. And should [the world] endure till mountain melt into mountain, and all the isles form one tableland; yet would it but expand the old battleplain.''[21] Turning to the doctrine of the mission of America to spread democracy throughout the world, Melville declared that the fate of the American Republic must be the same as that of its Roman predecessor. Democracy, thought the author of *Moby Dick*, is but a moment in history, not the end toward which all history runs. Yet Melville was not a pessimist, his critics to the contrary notwithstanding. Evil, he insisted, is both unconquerable and unconquering. A man can and must save his soul by fighting the evils of his day as Ahab on the deck of the "Pequod" pursued Moby Dick, well knowing that, though the chase must end in the defeat of the captain, yet it would not be a triumph for the white whale. If a man would be an individualist, taught Melville, if he would be free, let him stop running with the Christians to the Everlasting Arms, let him cease deluding himself with Emerson that the constitution of the universe is on his side. Melville in the middle years of the nineteenth century pitched overboard every one of the philosophies of individualism which dominated his age. Then the intellectuals of an era which proclaimed the ideal of liberty as an end in itself cast him out. His generation condemned Melville to nearly a score of years of living death as an outdoor clerk at the New York Customs House. He was defeated but he did not surrender. In *Billy Budd*, completed three months before his death in 1891, he challenged brilliantly and for the last time the democratic faith of America. Melville's was a troubled spirit which in coming to earth opened the door upon the wrong century.

Notes

[1]Quoted in Harry R. Warfel, Ralph H. Gabriel, and Stanley T. Williams, *The American Mind* (1937), p. 436.
[2]*Works* (Riverside ed., 1883), VI, p. 195.
[3]*Works* (Riverside ed., 1883), I, p. 113-114.

[4]*Johnson and Graham's Lessee* v. *William M'Intosh* & *Wheaton*, p. 543, 572.

[5]*Miscellaneous Writings* (1835), p. 74.

[6]*Works* (11th ed.), II, p. 40.

[7]*Works* (Centenary ed.), I, p. 41-42.

[8]*Commentaries on the Constitution of the United States* (Boston, Mass., 1877).

[9]*Works* (Centenary ed.), XI, p. 236.

[10]*Cannibals All* (Richmond, Va., 1857), p. 116.

[11]*Republican* (1820), p. 56.

[12]*Nature and Tendency of Free Institutions* (Cincinnati, Ohio, 1856), p. 1.

[13]*Works* (Centenary ed.), III, p. 215-216.

[14]*Works* (Centenary ed.), III, p. 216-217.

[15]Ibid., XI, p. 229.

[16]"The Nation," a hymn (1833).

[17]*Oration*, delivered in Boston, July 4, 1866.

[18]*Oration*, delivered at Avon, N.Y., July 4, 1827, printed by Bemis, Morse, and Ward, Canandaigua, N.Y.

[19]*Miscellaneous Writings* (1835), p. 86.

[20]"As a Strong Bird on Pinions Free," Commencement Poem, Dartmouth College, June 26, 1872.

[21]*Mardi* (Standard ed., 1922), p. 244-245.

2

American Democracy in the World Crisis

A little more than a hundred years ago a square-rigged, snub-nosed sailing ship stood down Boston harbor and turned her prow toward Europe—many weeks away. The Atlantic in those days was a broad ocean. On board was a young man, George Bancroft, just out of Harvard, journeying to Europe for advanced study. Bancroft was later to become the first historian to trace the origin and evolution of the American democratic ideal.

Bancroft left a nation that was new, undeveloped, and immature. Boston, when he sailed, was scarcely two centuries old. He sought acquaintance in Europe with a civilization that was more than a thousand years old, a land where crumbling ruins kept alive

SOURCE: This essay was originally presented as the concluding paper in a symposium held by the social science departments of Wheaton College at Norton, Massachusetts, October 4 & 5, 1940. Copyright 1940 by the Periwinkle Press, Norton, Massachusetts. Reprinted by permission of Katherine Burton.

17

memories of vanished ages. Cathedrals, monuments of the religion of the Middle Ages, towered above the cities. Bancroft, from a nation almost illiterate in music, heard for the first time Bach played by masters. European civilization was a rich tapestry in comparison with which American civilization was like homespun. Europeans, moreover, were not preoccupied with the past. They were pushing confidently forward. In vibrant universities scholars were pursuing learning in all its forms. Scientists were wresting from nature secrets to transform the world. Young Bancroft went to learn. Settling himself in a German university, he wrote: "I have come to the pure fountains of wisdom that I may drink of her unpolluted waters and be refreshed."

With all its crudities and immaturities Bancroft's America had a virile life of its own. Lean pioneers, armed with rifle and plow, were conquering a wilderness. They were building a nation almost equal in physical size to Europe and governed by free men. They were establishing a civilization on the principle of the freedom of the individual—freedom to think, to speak, and to worship according to conscience. For Bancroft's contemporaries freedom implied responsibility. They insisted that the free individual be responsible for his own destiny and that of his family, responsible for assuming a share in the management of a growing nation.

In the nineteenth century, Europe was the center of civilization, the hope of the world. Americans looked to Europe for learning, for standards of taste, for inspiration.

Today Europe and the world are in crisis. Our minds are absorbed with news of bombings, of military and naval forays, of the fall of nations. We wonder if Britain can hold out. We are startled by a treaty of alliance among three totalitarian powers aimed specifically at us. It makes certain two things: the wars in Europe and Asia are one war; the dictators have pointed the pistol at us. This is crisis enough. It justly commands our most earnest attention. Serious as it is, it is not so terrifying as another crisis that lies, half forgotten, behind the fighting.

It is the fate of our generation to watch the decline of the greatest civilization in the history of mankind, the civilization from which ours is sprung and from which George Bancroft and thousands of American successors have derived enlightenment and power. It was a terrible thing in the spring of 1940, when the trees and fields were covered with new green, to witness the death of France. France, we remembered, gave us Rheims, Millet, Pasteur. Before France died, however, Germany had already gone down, the Germany that had produced Goethe, Bach, Einstein. We would do well to look closely at the centralizing political and economic control so as to permit the nation to move swiftly and to strike powerfully in an emergency. It puts into the hands of the leader a sword whose destructiveness is beyond the wildest dreams of Caesar.

For all its seeming efficiency, however, totalitarianism is a sign of the decay of civilization. Wherever totalitarianism appears in a highly civilized nation, it means that the march forward has come to an end and that retreat has begun. Under totalitarianism the political state, centering in one man and no longer responsible to the people, becomes a leviathan. The head of the state may use the vast destructive power it has accumulated in artillery, tanks, and airplanes to annihilate rebels at home as well as to assail enemies abroad. We need expect no armed insurrections in conquered France or Czechoslovakia. A rabble armed with squirrel guns cannot stand against a tank. The leviathan state swallows up the individual. With its propaganda devices, constructed out of the knowledge made available by the science of psychology, the totalitarian state puts into the minds of its people the thoughts they are to think and on their tongues the words they are to speak. By so doing it drags in the dust the dignity of human nature. Totalitarianism is a symptom of the decay of civilization because it treats human beings with a contempt unsurpassed in history.

Nor is this antihumanism all. Totalitarianism, substituting force for reason, has transcended the moral law and has proclaimed the doctrine that a nation is a law unto itself. It has introduced a new religion—the worship of the nation or, better, of a mythical race with a supposed world destiny to perform. What is the essence of this new state or race worship that has so much to say about military virtues? It should be remembered that totalitarianism has been made possible by the energy—force—that science has put into the hands of men. And it came to pass in the middle years of the twentieth century that men bowed down before that force and worshipped it. The totalitarian powers have set up a tyranny on principles as ancient as Nebuchadnezzar and have called it a new world order. They have taken the road back toward barbarism.

The task that confronts our generation and will confront it so long as we shall live is the rehabilitation and the regeneration of civilization. The immediate job is to stop the military progress of the dictators. That enterprise is easier than the task that lies beyond.

Totalitarianism, with its worship of force, is, at bottom, a product of the ethical confusion that has manifested itself in the twentieth century. The rising prestige of science has been partly responsible for a relative decline in that of religion. As a result, the ancient religious foundations for a moral order have been shaken. We have not the time to go into the battles of recent decades between the proponents of relativism and those of absolutism in the realm of ethics. Suffice it to say that for a quarter of a century here in America the intellectual world has been plagued with confusion. Because religious authority had declined we were unable to define the good in such a way as to give us a sense of security. Totalitarianism, with its ethic that that which is expedient is right, is the logical product of an age of ethical confusion. If we are to preserve our own civilization and to aid in the rehabilitation of that of Europe, we must rediscover a morality that proclaims that some types of behavior are always wrong. As we face the present crisis we desperately need affirmations that we can trust. I think we can find them, if we look at the way of life that makes science possible.

We should remind ourselves of a strange paradox in totalitarianism, built on that energy made available by natural science. When the Nazi leaders forced totalitarianism upon the German people, science itself began to die. True, the Germans remained skillful engineers and technicians. But the evidence is overwhelming that pure science is declining. Nazi race anthropology is the product and symbol of this intellectual deterioration. Since modern civilization rests largely upon the knowledge won by pure science, this decline is an ominous portent of the future. Science is failing in Germany because the German totalitarian state has compelled the abandonment of the way of life that makes science possible. For, in the end, science rests on ethics. Four principles, absolute and unchangeable, provide the cornerstones that make not only science but all learning possible.

Learning is the harvest of reason. Force solves no scientific problems. We must respect the things of the mind, for our civilization is built upon them. We must honor the life of reason if we would save our lives. Science makes no compromise with anti-intellectualism.

Learning is the harvest of the free individual spirit. The mind, forbidden to enter certain areas, cannot discover new and unsuspected continents of knowledge. The mind, filled with a particular pattern of ideas hurled ceaselessly against it by the deadly rhythm of a propaganda machine, cannot open up new vistas of thought. Science makes no compromise with domination.

Learning is the harvest of responsible freedom. When the scholar falsifies his observations or results, learning dies. Science makes no compromise with dishonesty.

Learning is the harvest of mutual trust among honest men working for the general good. Science cannot be produced by one man alone, even if that man be a Newton or an Einstein. Science implies, and not many years ago had achieved, a worldwide republic of learning, a republic of men of good will cooperating in the service of mankind. Science makes no compromise with an ethic of suspicion, hatred, or force. When humanism dies, learning is laid in its grave.

What are these principles? They are a restatement of an American democratic faith now more than a century old. They inhere in democratic idealism wherever men have followed it. This faith of democracy included and still includes the doctrine that underneath society are basic and enduring principles of behavior that make society possible and that apply to nations as well as to individual men. This faith includes the doctrines of freedom and responsibility for the individual. It sets in the sky the vision of a world order made up of free men each of whom so governs his conduct as to make it accord with the principles underlying the group life of mankind. In essence our faith is the belief that the goal of life is the fellowship of humane, free, and cultivated men.

This is a fighting faith. Ideals also are weapons. The colleges and universities of America must become centers of idealism —strong points in the long, hard campaign to rehabilitate civilization. And that campaign must begin in our own land.

We are fortunate among the long succession of generations of men. Our years have been set in a grim epoch that offers rare opportunities for living. It is our opportunity as Americans to make our humanistic, democratic faith the foundation of an organized world.

3

Spiritual Origins of American Culture

The Nazi challenge to Western civilization has set Americans to searching their own minds to discover the nature of their philosophy. The quest has been speeded by the growing understanding that ideas are instruments for effecting desired ends and weapons for combating adversaries. Americans have long used the word, democracy, to describe a way of life in the realm both of political and of social behavior that they consider desirable. But democracy, like many other words, has accumulated such a variety of meanings and emotional associations that it has been deprived of that precision which makes for understanding.

Those ideas which we have come to associate with democracy bordered on the radical in seventeenth-century colonial America.

SOURCE: This essay was read before a Conference on Education and the Faith of America at the Packer Collegiate Institute on April 12, 1945, and published in December 1945 as Hazen Pamphlet No. 14, p. 5-17. Copyright 1945 by the Packer Collegiate Institute. Reprinted with permission of the Institute.

The liberal thought of the Revolutionary period in the third quarter of the eighteenth century established many democratic ideas firmly in American thinking and gave to the world that great charter of democracy, the Declaration of Independence. But it is significant that the party of Thomas Jefferson, even as late as the opening days of the nineteenth century, called itself the Republican party. The word democracy did not achieve the full stature that it has in our day till the nineteenth century was well advanced. An analysis of the ideas that were thought of as democratic in the days of Andrew Jackson and of Ralph Waldo Emerson is a useful starting point for an exploration of the spiritual origins of our culture.

The Meaning of Democracy

Democracy had for the citizens of the mid-nineteenth century two quite distinct but interrelated meanings. It was thought of as a way of acting politically in both the creating and the management of government. This may be called, for want of a better term, realistic democracy. In their practice of the political art Americans have from the Revolution onward displayed a genius for practicality. They have produced few systematic political philosophers; their great contribution to world political thought has been in the creation of institutions that were workable and have worked. It is this quality of the American mind that helps to explain the paradox, that though the United States is one of the younger nations, its people today live under a form of government that is older than that of any important power save Britain. Two characteristics of American realistic democracy help to explain its success: a rejection sooner or later of whatever smacks of the doctrinaire and a healthy skepticism about human nature. No American political leader in his lifetime has ever inspired blind devotion; without exception our leaders have been watched with suspicion and criticized with vigor. This criticism has very frequently been on grounds of the practical results of actions taken.

But there has been from the beginning of our national history another background for political criticism, namely, that found in a pattern of almost universally accepted values. The second meaning of the word democracy in the days of Jackson and Emerson may be found in the use of the word to describe a collection of ideals that could be used as standards by which to judge action in the arena of affairs. These ideals were also gathered together in the word "civilization." They expressed the spiritual side of American culture. By the middle of the nineteenth century they had fixed themselves so firmly in American thought that they had an authority akin to that of an established religion. Christianity in a variety of denominational expressions had great prestige and influence in this middle period but many Americans challenged the older orthodoxies and sought to establish new liberalisms, some of which owed much to the Enlightenment philosophy of the eighteenth century. This separation between liberal and conservative wings in the realm of religious doctrine had, however, no counterpart in that domain of basic values which was the very center of American civilization in the mid-nineteenth century. These values were the same whether expressed in the language of Puritanism, of evangelical Protestantism, of the Catholicism of Bishop England or of Isaac Hecker, of the Unitarianism of William Ellery Channing, of the transcendentalism of Emerson and Thoreau, or the secular idealism of the young Abraham Lincoln. It should be remembered that for this generation, which did not know the naturalisms which were later to be created out of materials collected from post-Darwinian science, there were other similarities worth noting. If the ancient world of the educated man was Greece and Rome, the antiquity which had living force for all Americans was that of the Near East as set forth in the Old and New Testaments. And every American, no matter what his belief, understood the basic outline of that Christian thought which was the heritage of Western civilization. We now turn to a consideration of those values which, when taken together, mid-nineteenth-century Americans called the democratic way of life.

May I direct for a moment your attention to a scene on the desert of central Nevada in 1849. It was the first week in October. A trail lay like a ribbon carelessly dropped on the rolling plain, whose parched soil was only half concealed by straggling sage brush. Here and there in the distance mountains lifted irregular peaks into a cloudless sky. A lone, canvas-covered wagon drawn by two pairs of weary oxen moved along the trace which was strewn on either side with the wrecks of other wagons and with the carcasses of animals that had given out. A young man, his face lined with anxiety, drove the team. His wife walked ahead alone. Their infant daughter was in the wagon. Two other young men—strangers who had attached themselves to this party—were scouting far in advance.

This little group brought up the rear of the great overland trek to California in the year 1849. They were common people—this man and wife—named Royce. The young husband planned to open a store in one of the new towns of the California frontier. They were of good stock. A son, born to them later in California and whom they named Josiah, became in the opening years of the twentieth century one of the half dozen most important American thinkers. Josiah Royce's Philosophy of Loyalty was the last great nineteenth-century argument for idealism.

In the first week in October 1849, the Royce party moved eastward. They were in retreat. Two days before, they had missed a side trail leading off from the main trace and so had passed by the last water hole on the eastern margin of the dread Carson desert. When they had discovered their mistake, they were almost in despair. They had turned back to find the oasis where they could give their animals grass and replenish the water casks now almost empty. They were filled with fear, for their animals were flagging and the season was dangerously late.

It is a commonplace that crisis brings into action the deeper forces in the character of an individual. A nation is but a company of individuals. And the characteristics of a national civilization can only be observed in the character and behavior of individuals. Sarah Eleanor Royce and her husband were not typical of all mid-nineteenth-century Americans. But they were not far from the norm. They were engaged in an individualistic enterprise, young people seeking with courage and high hopes those opportunities which only the American frontier could offer. As a family group they depended on themselves. Like the great majority of Americans of their day, they lived in immediate contact with nature. Sarah Royce later recorded an experience she had as, filled with anxiety, she walked in front of the team whose heads drooped lower with each passing hour. Her account opens a window on the mind of the common American of the middle period of the nineteenth century.

Naturally, almost inevitably, her thought ran back to the Bible. "My imagination acted intensely," she said. "I seemed to see Hagar in the wilderness, walking away from the dried up bushes, and seating herself in the hot sand. I seemed to become Hagar myself, and when my little one from the wagon behind me called out, ... I stopped, gave her some (water), noted that there were only a few gallons left, then mechanically pressed on again, alone, repeating over and over the words, 'Let me not see the death of the child'. Just in the heat of noonday we came to where the sage bushes were closer together; a fire, left by campers or Indians, had spread some distance leaving beds of ashes, and occasionally charred skeletons of bushes to make the scene more dreary.

"Smoke was still sluggishly curling up here and there, but no fire was visible; when suddenly just before me to the right a bright flame sprang up at the foot of a small bush, ran rapidly up it, leaped from one little branch to another till all for a few seconds were ablaze together, then went out, leaving nothing but a few ashes and a little smouldering trunk. It was a small incident, easily accounted for, but to my then overwrought fancy it made more vivid the illusion of being a wanderer in a far off, old-time desert, and myself witnessing a wonderful phenomenon. For a few moments I stood with bowed head (before the burning bush), worshipping the God of Horeb, and I was strengthened thereby."

Before the end of the day the Royce party found the oasis they had missed. They paused to rest and to refresh the exhausted oxen. But they could not stop long. The Carson desert, hot and waterless, was still before them. And beyond that lay the high Sierras, into whose passes October snow was already drifting and threatening to block the road to California and to safety.

"There was no alternative," Sarah Royce remarked later. "The only thing to be done was to go steadily on, determined to do and to endure to the utmost." In this story of common folk on the American frontier may be found all the elements of that basic pattern of ideas which Walt Whitman once called the American democratic faith.

The Basic Ideas of the Democratic Faith

What were these ideas that came to focus in the first half of the nineteenth century? The first was the concept of *the free, rational, and responsible individual*; the individual capable by virtue of his reason of making wise and right decisions; the individual free to make for better or worse his choices; free to think his own thoughts and to express publicly his matured convictions; free to worship with Ralph Waldo Emerson the Over-Soul that pervaded all nature, or with Herman Melville the unfathomable Mystery, or with Sarah Eleanor Royce the ancient God of Horeb. The Royces were free to go to California to take advantage of the opportunities of a new community. But, as they faced the Carson desert, they were aware that the responsibility for the outcome of their enterprise rested wholly upon them.

Sarah Royce symbolized the second concept of this old democratic faith when she bowed for a moment reverently before the burning bush. This second concept was the conviction that, as a building is supported by its framework of timbers or girders, so *human society is supported by a framework of fixed principles*. Sarah Royce called them the laws of God before which all men are equal, and she summarized them in two commands to the individual, to love God and his neighbor. The intellectual descendants of that eighteenth-century liberal, Thomas Jefferson, called them the laws of Nature and expressed them in the concept of natural rights—the right of the individual to life, to liberty, and to the pursuit of happiness. Both the religious and the secular formulations were, in fact, a belief in a fundamental law underlying human life, a law as universal as mankind, a law whose principles provide the cornerstone for the good life. Emerson declared that moral principle is the essence of Nature. Chancellor James Kent insisted that the judge in applying the statute in the case of the offender must in his reasoning and his decision strike down into that ethical substratum on which all human law ultimately rests. This doctrine of a fundamental law created that second belief of the mid-nineteenth century that the law, when found by honorable and independent judges, is and should be certain. The men of the middle period, whether they subscribed to some Christian orthodoxy, to the rationalistic humanism that had come down from the Enlightenment, or to Emerson's transcendentalism, united in the conviction that, when men or their rulers disregard the basic ethical principles that underlie human life, decay will set in. Then civilization, losing its vision of the good, will degenerate into barbarism.

The word barbarism suggests the third of the four concepts of that democratic faith that provided the frame of thought for Americans of a century ago. This concept was *the idea of progress*. The sense of and the belief in progress so pervaded American thought in the middle of the nineteenth century that Americans were scarcely aware of it as an article of faith. The Royces, trekking westward to better themselves, expressed the idea of progress in its simplest form. They saw a richer future ahead for themselves, and still greater opportunities for their children than they had enjoyed. Their simple philosophy of American history was that each generation would start life by standing on the shoulders of the generation before. So Americans would climb the slopes of a rugged upland—on and on toward the heights of the future. But the idea of progress was, perhaps, best expressed in that definition of civilization universally accepted by mid-nineteenth-century Americans. Sarah Eleanor Royce and Henry Thoreau would have agreed that that quality which chiefly distinguishes the civilized man from the barbarian is the better understanding and observance on the part of the former of the fundamental ethical principles which underlie human institutions. Civilization is a manifestation and a proof of progress, of material and intellectual progress, of course, but at the bottom of ethical progress. For civilization is the fruit of an understanding of the fundamental moral law and of the founding of human institutions upon it.

The fourth concept of the democratic faith of the middle of the nineteenth century was that of *national destiny*. This was not the nationalism that expresses itself in the vision of a government equipped with mighty armies and navies to enforce its will in the world. The nationalism of the democratic faith of the 1840s and 1850s was primarily the concept of a nation as a company of men and women whose destinies were united by the political and cultural ties that bound them together. Americans felt that they, as free men and hence the ultimate rulers of the United States, had a responsibility to hold up their government before the world as a witness to the fact that, when common people are given political liberty, they can govern themselves. Those Americans looked upon themselves, not without a certain naivete, as the chief exemplars in the world of the democratic way of life. The bombast in their expression of this conviction sometimes made them a little ridiculous. But if the Fourth of July orator too often shouted about American greatness to compensate for a feeling of cultural inferiority, there were others confident and assured, like the quiet Emerson, who understood both the uncouthness and the strength of young America. That strength was the ideal of liberty founded on the natural and the moral law, and the belief that it was the nation's mission to stand before the world as a witness for that ideal.

The civilization of the mid-nineteenth century had its shoddy and its vicious aspects. It was a time of mob violence against unpopular minorities. Henry Thoreau looked about him in New England and saw in the rising industrialism the triumph of greed expressed in the exploitation of the men, women, and children who worked for twelve-hour days in the mills. Thoreau also was one of the prophets of the mid-nineteenth-century democratic idealism which stood over against the political and social evils of the time. When young Thoreau walked with Emerson across the fields and through the woods to Walden Pond, the two talked often of the prime duty of the political state. This was nothing less than the production of strong, humane, self-reliant, and self-disciplined individuals who were governed ultimately by the moral law and whose great goal was progress in the incorporation of that law in American living. For these two in Massachusetts as for Lincoln in Illinois, the four doctrines of the democratic faith represented a formulation of values by which both individuals and the nation could test and govern behavior. It was not an expression of how Americans lived; it was a pattern of ideals which gave meaning and dignity to American life, ideals for which in the 1860s hundreds of thousands of sons of the Republic gave their lives. "The movements of the late secession war, and their results," wrote Whitman in 1872, "show that popular democracy, whatever its faults and dangers, practically justifies itself beyond the proudest claims and wildest hopes of its enthusiasts. Probably no future age can know, but I well know how the gist of this fiercest and most resolute of the world's war-like contentions resided exclusively in the unnamed, unknown rank and file; and how the brunt of its labor of death was, to all essential purposes, volunteer'd. The People, of their own choice, fighting, dying, for their idea . . ."

Three Strands of a Tradition

Whence came these ideas and attitudes that stirred Whitman to admiration? They grew partly out of the conditions of life on that American frontier which in the seventeenth century began its westward progression from the very beaches of the Atlantic. Where, as in the seventeenth- and eighteenth-century frontier, men were few and the original homeland months away across a dangerous ocean, where the dangers of the forest were ominous and the task of subduing the wilderness almost insuperable, human life took on a significance almost unknown in the Old World. The cruel punishments of Europe died out. Labor took on a new dignity and men came to be valued for what they could contribute to the common effort. Where, as in the nineteenth century, an agrarian population was thinly scattered over vast areas of the continental interior, the home with its intimate personal ties emerged as the basic unit in social organization and individualism, liberty, and equality were inevitable. In an age when common men drove back the wilderness and replaced it with a nation ever developing and expanding, the belief in progress would not be denied. Jefferson in writing the Declaration of Independence used the phrases of Locke and of the *philosophes* of the Enlightenment but he expressed convictions born of a great adventure already a century and a half old in a new world.

Yet the very fact that Jefferson found it useful to write the Declaration in terms of Lockean philosophy suggests that the men of the American frontiers were conditioned by and were bearers of a tradition. This tradition ran back not only to the great English philosopher of the seventeenth century but past him through the Middle Ages, through Rome and Greece to Asia Minor, a tradition that could make Sarah Eleanor Royce in a moment of despair pause before the burning bush to worship the God of Horeb. There were many strands within this tradition; three of these are of particular importance in the development of American thinking. I shall try to suggest them as they were expressed in the lives of three seventeenth- and eighteenth-century Americans.

Pause with me for a moment in a winter forest in eastern Massachusetts in the middle 1630s. Snow covered the ground and the crude bark huts of an Indian town. The picture cannot be reconstructed in all its details but the essentials are clear. It was Massasoit's village of Wampanoags inhabited by a handful of copper-skinned people still living in the stone age. A white man, tired after a winter journey of several days alone through the wilderness, came out of the woods and made his way hesitatingly to the chief's hut. Roger Williams, exile, had come to spend the winter with the red men of the woods and to live with them in the noisy, reeking intimacy of their filthy smoke holes. He was only seven years out of the University of Cambridge where he had gotten his B.A. in 1627 and had taken orders in 1629. He was one of that band of Puritans who had given up that brilliant and cultivated England where Shakespeare had died only yesterday, and, fleeing ecclesiastical persecution, had founded what they hopefully called a "holy Commonwealth" in the New World. But Williams had proved too independent a thinker for the governors of Massachusetts, with the result that now he was glad to sit beside the fire of the headman of a forest tribe. When Williams departed in the spring to found his colony at Providence, he had established between himself and the redskins who lived in the neighborhood of Narragansett Bay bonds of enduring friendship. Williams was on his own as during that winter he went from tribe to tribe engaged in a forest diplomacy that would guarantee security to the colony he intended to found. He was on his own in the spring when he picked the site of Providence and prepared to receive his friends and colonists from Salem. This episode suggests the contributions of Puritanism to American democracy.

Three things stand out. Williams and his fellow Puritans were impressed with the extent and the toughness of evil in the world and the obligation of men to struggle against it. The Puritan, with Augustine, saw the heart of man as fundamentally corrupt by inheritance from the fallen Adam. Children according to this philosophy were by definition little vipers. Williams, with John Winthrop and John Cotton, fought evil in England, and later in America Williams alone fought what he considered to be evil in the Massachusetts Bay Colony. Opposed to evil for the Puritan, as for the Middle Ages before him, was the law of God, the fundamental law which contains the pattern of discipline for men and society. Obedience to this fundamental law was the first duty of all subjects of the English king no matter what Charles I or his archbishop might say. Obedience to this fundamental law, moreover, is an obligation of the individual conscience, for as Roger Williams faced alone the dangers of the winter wilderness, so man confronts his God alone. From Puritanism more than from any other source the American democratic faith of the middle of the nineteenth century derived its emphasis upon the fundamental moral law and upon the doctrine of the self-disciplined individual. Williams, whose social philosophy was half a century ahead of Locke, emphasized in his own thinking and in his colony the importance of freedom for the individual and the necessity for some form of compact among the people in the setting up of a government. "It is evident," he remarked, "that such governments as are by them erected and established have no more power, nor for longer time, than the civil power of people consenting and agreeing shall betrust them with."

A century and more ran by. In the spring of 1757 the fruit trees came into bloom in the hamlet of Mount Holly in southern New

Jersey some miles on the king's highway northeast of Philadelphia. Before a tidy village house a youngish man of thirty-seven, clad in plain clothes and wearing a brimmed hat that contrasted with the cocked hats of the day, lifted his bulging saddle bags to the back of his horse, bade an affectionate goodbye to his wife and daughter, and disappeared down the road stretching toward the city which Penn had founded. John Woolman, Quaker, was setting out upon his second and most important journey into the South. He carried with him a certificate of religious concern from the Burlington, New Jersey, Quarterly Meeting of Friends. He intended to visit with the Quakers in the Shenandoah Valley and at other settlements in the southern colonies. Friend John, having reached the conclusion that Negro slavery was incompatible with the Quaker faith, was acting on the dictates of his conscience. He was no warped extremist. He was a man of business, of letters, and of profound religious conviction. He filled his pockets with coins, not only to pay for his hospitality in southern homes, but so that he could be sure to make change if his host did not have cash available. Woolman, as a matter of principle, planned to defy the tradition of southern hospitality that no guest could give money. He would accept no hospitality made possible by the work of slaves. "I believed," he wrote in 1757 exactly a hundred years before the Dred Scott decision, "that liberty was the natural right of all men equally." He was a genial and friendly man and achieved the triumph not only of speaking his mind to the southern Friends but of paying his way among them while retaining their respect and good will. The triumph was not entirely personal. Woolman represented the very genius of Quakerism, and Friends, both in the North and South, knew that to be the case. It was Quaker philosophy more than Woolman that caused the Virginia and North Carolina Friends to join with their brethren in Pennsylvania and New Jersey in reconsidering the matter of slavery.

What did Quakerism contribute to American democratic thinking? The Quakers gathered on the Sabbath in their meeting house to sit in silence waiting for the voice of God that spoke in their hearts. God, they thought, speaks to humble men and women, as well as to the learned and the great. His children are all equal in His sight. If God has such regard for men of low degree, the followers of George Fox argued, could Englishmen do less? The Quakers emphasized the natural dignity of men founded on the fact that their all-powerful Creator is willing to pause to speak to the heart of the least among them. William Penn based his Indian policy on the principle that the red man of the forest was to be treated with the respect and the consideration due an immortal human being. In the eighteenth century the Quakers initiated in the American colonies that movement to end the slavery of the Negro which in the nineteenth century was to become a great crusade. If Puritanism gave to American democracy an emphasis on the fundamental law and the disciplined individual, Quakerism stressed individual liberty, the dignity and worth of man and universal brotherhood. Other Christian groups did the same, for the ideas are very old. But the Quakers, widely distributed in America, gave these ancient concepts a particular emphasis. From Quakerism came an inspired humanitarianism which reached its eighteenth-century flowering in the life and writings of John Woolman. It was his humanitarian spirit that softened the individualism of the nineteenth century by adding to the responsibilities of the strong man the duty of aiding his less fortunate brother. ''We have no cause to promote,'' wrote Woolman, ''but the cause of . . . . universal love.''

In the middle years of the twentieth century, Americans erected on the banks of the Potomac a marble memorial to Thomas Jefferson, and placed in it a statue of the planter from Albemarle County, Virginia. On its walls in bronze they set words which he wrote, not only on paper but in his life. One evening at dinner in Washington a member of the Polish embassy told me that the Jefferson Memorial was the place in the national capital he liked best to go. Whenever he could, he took his European friends to the shrine to see the figure and to read the bronze tablets. For him it expressed the essence of American idealism, it was America standing as a witness for democracy before the world. Jefferson was a farmer, a statesman, an architect, and a philosopher. He was also a man of religion. He had little use for the conventional creeds of his day or for outward formal manifestations of his faith. For him religion was a very private thing and he once remarked to a man who aspired to be his biographer that the nature of a man's religion could best be discovered in his way of living. The planter from Albemarle whose Monticello library was rich in the classics of the ancient world had taken the trouble to put together in a little book the moral teachings of the Founder of Christianity. Jefferson was one of the outstanding American representatives of that phase of liberal social thought known as the eighteenth-century Enlightenment. The core of this philosophy was faith in God as the Author of Nature, in man as possessed of infinite capacities to advance on the road toward perfection, and in reason as the instrument by which man could know Nature and its Author, and by which man could move forward in unending progress. What the Enlightenment, stemming from the science of Newton and the philosophy of Locke, contributed to the American democratic faith besides its doctrine of progress may be found in those words of Jefferson which twentieth-century Americans put on the walls of his memorial.

"We hold these truths to be self-evident: that all men are created equal, that they are endowed by their Creator with certain inalienable rights, among these are life, liberty, and the pursuit of happiness, that to secure these rights governments are instituted among men. . . ."

"I am not an advocate for frequent change in laws and constitutions. But laws and institutions must go hand in hand with the progress of the human mind. As that becomes more developed, more enlightened, as new discoveries are made,

new truths discovered. . . . institutions must advance also to
keep pace with the times. . . ."
    "Almighty God hath created the mind free. . . ."
    "I have sworn upon the Altar of God eternal hostility
against every form of tyranny over the mind of man."

There is the American democratic faith—the fundamental law,
the free and responsible individual who is the equal of his fellows
before the law, the hope of progress, and the sense of high destiny.
We in the middle of the twentieth century, like the Royce party in
the middle of the nineteenth, have come face to face with crises.
For us in these days the words of Sarah Eleanor Royce, as the
weary party turned westward for the last time toward the difficult
and dangerous mountains, have a peculiar relevance. "There was
no alternative," she said. "The only thing to be done was to go
steadily on determined to do and to endure to the utmost."

4

The Enlightenment Tradition

In the middle period of the twentieth century, Americans erected on the banks of the Potomac in the city of Washington a memorial of white marble. It suggests the Pantheon in ancient Rome but its more recent inspiration was the Rotunda which Thomas Jefferson had designed as the intellectual center and the architectural climax of his University of Virginia. Within the walls of the memorial stands a statue of that country squire who wished to be remembered chiefly for having founded the university and for having written the Declaration of Independence and the Virginia statute establishing religious liberty. Not far from this memorial stand two

SOURCE: This paper was one of a series of eighteen lectures given at the Jewish Theological Seminary of America in New York City, under the auspices of The Institute for Religious and Social Studies. Sixteen of these lectures were published under the title *Wellsprings of the American Spirit*, ed. F. Ernest Johnson (New York, 1948), p. 39-47 (copyright 1948 by The Institute for Religious and Social Studies). Reprinted with permission of the Institute.

others, that to Lincoln and the simple shaft which commemorates the name of Washington. The date of the Jeffersonian memorial is not without interest. It came late—almost a century and a half after the death of the master of Monticello. It was built to celebrate a man of agriculture by the citizens of a highly complex industrial age. Nor was the memorial the expression of the attitude of a minority group. It was evidence that Thomas Jefferson at long last had taken his place among the small group of American folk heroes of the first rank. But the event had more than significance for the memory of an individual man. Both Jefferson and Washington were men of the eighteenth century. But Jefferson alone in his outlook and in his contribution to thought and civilization can be called one of that small world company of *philosophes* who were the leaders of the Enlightenment. In raising Jefferson to a place of the highest rank in the American pantheon, mid-twentieth-century Americans were doing homage to the Enlightenment. The reasons for this belated turning to the Enlightenment, if such it was, are worth exploring.

As the eighteenth century gave way to the nineteenth, a young clergyman in New York City busied himself with the writing of a book, one among many that came from his hurrying pen. Samuel Miller, not yet thirty-five, was associated with two colleagues in a collegiate pastorate of the three Presbyterian churches: Wall Street, Brick, and Rutgers Street. In addition to preaching and writing he was wont to deliver several addresses each week, to make many pastoral calls, and to carry on a voluminous correspondence. In 1803, this dynamic individual who sought to carry the élan of the eighteenth century into the nineteenth, published a two-volume work to which he gave the somewhat misleading title, *Brief Retrospect of the Eighteenth Century*. From a pastor's study in which the influence of John Calvin was a living force Samuel Miller looked back on what Voltaire in France and Gibbon in England had called the Age of Enlightenment. Miller agreed with their nomenclature. Neither Benjamin Franklin nor Thomas Jefferson ever equaled the rhetoric of Miller as he depicted the foundations of the century just gone.

At the close of the seventeenth century, the stupendous mind of Newton and the penetrating genius of Locke, had laid their systems of matter and 'of mind before the world. Like pioneers in an arduous siege, they had many formidable obstacles to remove—many labyrinths to explore—and the power of numberless enemies to overcome. But they accomplished the mighty enterprise. With cautious, but firm and dauntless steps, they made their way to the entrenchments of fortified error; they scaled her walls; forced her confident and blustering champions to retreat; and planted the standard of truth, where the banner of ignorance and of falsehood had so long waved.

Rather good for a Calvinist.

Newton and Locke were of the essence of Jefferson's thought. And, if Newton disclosed the reality of matter in motion, Franklin, completing a line of investigation begun by Farraday, disclosed a century after Newton the reality of electricity in motion. The Enlightenment was the outgrowth in popular thought of the work of the two great seventeenth-century Englishmen. Franklin and Jefferson were evidence not only that the Enlightenment, as a phase of thought, had made its way to English provincial society west of the Atlantic but that eighteenth-century American culture was capable of contributing to it figures of world importance, one in science and the other in social and political philosophy.

Samuel Miller in his book caught the essential mood of the Enlightenment. Newton had applied mathematical logic—the eighteenth century called it reason—to the mechanical problems of the heavens. Observation had verified his results. The success of Newtonian physics gave rise to an élan that was a blend of triumph and of confident hope. The eighteenth-century man was like a climber making his way at dawn up a mountain flank through the ground fog at the base until suddenly he found himself in the clean air and clear light of early morning. He felt that he had left superstition behind and below him. He was convinced that reason was an instrument that would ultimately enable men to discover the inmost mind of God, conceived of as a Great Engineer and as the Author of Nature. Within less than two centuries after Franklin's kite brought electricity to earth from the storm cloud, reason has enabled men to lay hold upon the elemental electrical energy of the cosmos. Two centuries are but a short time in the history of the race. The buoyant optimism of the Enlightenment has been justified. Men have, in fact, made a beginning in understanding the basic technique of the Cosmic Engineer.

John Locke turned his thought to the problems of man in society. He emphasized the individual man as endowed with reason and with certain natural rights that reason can discover. He pictured the human mind as, at birth, a *tabula rasa* which, as the years pass, gets its configuration and character from the sensations that flow in upon it from the encircling environment. Man, thought Locke and the Enlightenment after him, could manipulate this environment through the use of reason and, by so doing, effect improvement, perhaps perfection, in the quality of men. Locke and his American disciple, Jefferson, thought of this manipulation primarily in political terms. Men of reason by governing themselves could shape conditions to further the general progress. The idea of progress was central to the eighteenth century.

The Enlightenment produced, inevitably, not only a cosmology, the concept of a machine universe functioning perfectly, and a social philosophy, the doctrines of natural rights of environmentalism and progress, but also a religion, the religion of nature. There were many and varied expressions of this religion of nature in the old world and the new. Philip Freneau, lover of the sea, and fiery pamphleteer and poet of the American Revolutionary epoch, managed to compress not only the religion but with it the cosmology and the social philosophy of the Enlightenment into a single verse:

> Religion, such as nature taught,
> With all divine perfection suits;
> Had all mankind this system sought
> Sophists would cease their vain disputes,
> And from this source would nations know
> All that can make their heaven below.

Men of the mid-twentieth century look back a little wistfully upon the Enlightenment. So much has happened and so much been learned since Freneau wrote. The world has seemed to grow old. A weary sophistication has replaced that exuberant optimism of two centuries ago. Fear spreads among a conquering generation.

In such an age we rebuild Williamsburg and develop it into an important center of research in the eighteenth century. We write popular and scholarly biographies of Jefferson. And we plan a gigantic publication of all the writings of this latest addition to the galaxy of our greatest folk heroes. Yet to the men of the middle of the twentieth century the doctrine of the perfectibility of human nature seems childishly naive. Not even John Calvin had a deeper sense than we of the extent and the toughness of evil in the world. Are we then inclined to run away from an uneasy present and to clutch at an optimism made romantic by distance? I think there is more than this in the building of the Jefferson Memorial. There are enduring values in the Enlightenment. There is even a kinship between the mid-twentieth century and the eighteenth in America.

The Enlightenment emphasized the individual man. And for this emphasis it was indebted in part to a long Christian tradition of which, in fact, for all its religion of nature, it was a part. It was the individual who had natural rights which the state was created to secure. It was the individual who had reason which entitled him to the dignity of participating in his own government. The eighteenth-century man, following the seventeenth-century philosophers, thought of government in terms of a social contract. Rousseau brought this concept to its full development. In the early years of the Enlightenment social thinkers in Western Europe, under the influence of Newton and of the idea of the cosmos as an infinitely perfect machine, had thought of men as governed by natural law in almost a physical sense. The great German, Immanuel Kant, had moved away from the materialistic tendencies of the early post-Newtonian thinkers. For natural law in a physical sense he had substituted the idea that the substructure of society is made up of the laws of freedom or, as he preferred to call them, moral laws. For Kant the central social fact was the free individual. Kant's theory of history was that it is the struggle to achieve a civil society in which the individual is conceived of as an end in himself and in which the moral law replaces force as the supreme authority. The specific ideas of Kant were not important in America until the nineteenth century. But the drift of American thinking in the second half of the eighteenth century showed many similarities to that of the German philosopher.

Actions are usually more expressive than words of the ruling ideas of an age and place. An episode that took place in 1782 at Newburgh, where Washington had established headquarters, illuminates better than any formal pronouncement the character of American eighteenth-century thought. The Revolution was nearly over. Americans looked upon the struggle just ending as a war to preserve the natural rights of men. Not long before, the Commonwealth of Massachusetts had written the doctrine of natural rights into a new constitution. Yorktown in 1781 had brought the fighting to a victorious conclusion, but the peace had not yet been secured. The new Articles of Confederation had drawn the outlines of a confederacy but had failed to establish a central authority that could command the respect of Americans. The Congress of the Confederation, made up for the most part of second-rate politicians whose vision seldom extended beyond the boundaries of their respective states, was without funds or the power to raise the funds to pay the officers who had led the armies of the Revolution through defeat to victory. Many of these were compelled to see their families plunged into want and suffering humiliating hardships. The angry murmurs of men unjustly treated by their government grew in volume until an anonymous paper passed from hand to hand announcing the date of a meeting at which a plan would be presented for a march on the Congress and a demand for justice by organized and armed men before they were stripped of their power by the demobilization of the army. Washington found himself faced with his greatest crisis outside the field of battle.

He was not taken by surprise. Not long before, a spokesman for a group of men who felt that governmental weakness was bringing the country to chaos and disaster had approached him with the suggestion that it was his patriotic duty while he still wore the sword to become the strong man who would lead his demoralized countrymen to peace and prosperity. He had administered to this representative of evil a sharp rebuke. Now he commanded his officers to assemble in the old church at Newburgh. Entering at the designated hour, he stood before them with all the prestige of the victorious chieftain. He called upon them to lay aside their arms and to put their faith in an impotent, drab, and timorous congress:

> Let me conjure you in the name of our common country, as you value your own sacred honor, as you respect the rights of humanity and as you regard the military and national character of America to express your . . . detestation of the man who wishes under any specious pretences to overturn the liberties of our country, and who wickedly attempts to open the floodgates of civil discord and deluge our rising empire with blood.

As significant as Washington's appeal is the fact that his officers heeded his voice. Their sense of the importance of the rights of humanity and of their obligation to secure these rights triumphed over the temptation to appeal to force even in a just cause. In the following year Washington, at the zenith of his power and influence, presented himself to a congress of mediocrities and surrendered the commission their more illustrious predecessors had given him.

The military leader of the Revolution was a man of faith—faith in the reason and in the rectitude of the common men of eighteenth-century America. No man of his generation knew his fellow countrymen better. As commanding general, Washington had seen them carry through deadly encounters with a stout courage. He had seen them also turn poltroons and run away with scarcely a shot. He had seen them loot the homes of their private enemies. He had watched them desert when the common cause hung in the balance. He had lived with them in camp as they remained steadfast and loyal through the long winter of Valley Forge. Washington knew the strength and the weakness, the stupidities and the wisdom of the everyday American. His thought and theirs were shaped by the same social philosophy. He was willing to trust the nation in the hands of its citizens. On this faith American democratic theory and practice are founded. Behind that faith was the belief in the reality of the rights of humanity and the ultimate efficacy of the moral law.

The men of the Enlightenment thought naturally in terms of universals as well as in terms of free individuals. They spoke of universal natural rights that they conceived to flow from the nature and dignity of man himself. It was the fashion in Europe and even in some quarters in the United States in that uneasy period between the two great world wars to think primarily of men in terms of their organization into rival nation-states. Tribalism in the twentieth century grew to terrifying proportions. There were some, even in America, who denied that the concept of humanity, of man in general, had any utility and who affirmed that nations or races are the ultimates in society. The so-called realists of the 1920s dismissed contemptuously the idea of universal values. They emphasized the particular, especially that particular power structure, the nation-state.

From such a philosophy it was but a step to the doctrine that in the relations between these modern supertribes the only reality is the never-ending struggle for power. Out of such doctrines grew the disaster which recently engulfed us. And from this holocaust our country has emerged possessed of power surpassing anything the world has known—and with that power a gnawing sense of apprehension as to what the consequences of that power may be. It is fitting and a hopeful sign that in such an age we should enshrine in a chaste and simple temple in our national capital the memory of a great champion of the rights of all men. And to put on the walls of that shrine the words of the Squire of Monticello: ''Almighty God hath created the mind free. . . . I have sworn upon the altar of God hostility against every form of tyranny over the mind of man.'' The men of the Enlightenment believed that there are values of universal validity throughout mankind. This doctrine also came from ancient Palestinian tradition. It was an expression, in an age when many parts of the world were little known to Europeans or Americans, of the concept of men as forming for some purposes a single world community. Because we desperately need this concept in the modern world we turn our eyes back to the eighteenth century, when the concept was the beginning of social thinking.

The debt of twentieth-century America to that small provincial eighteenth-century community scattered along the Atlantic seaboard needs no emphasis. Since Freneau wrote of religion and nature we have passed through the romanticism of the first half of the nineteenth century, the crude materialism of the age of the robber barons and the disillusioned naturalism of the post-Versailles decade. In the 1930s we discovered with Freud that psychological reality, and with Pareto that social reality, lie in part in the irrational. We saw in totalitarian mass movements anti-intellectualism grow into a spurious crusade to bring salvation to the modern age. Tribalism, anti-intellectualism, the worship of naked power—these were devils that entered and threatened to take possession of the edifice of Western civilization. At heavy cost they have been, for the moment, at least partially subdued. Now a generation that has concluded the greatest of all wars takes stock. What vestiges of romanticism remained before the invasion of Poland are gone. A stark realism born of fighting on all the continents and all the oceans characterizes the modern mind. Skepticism goes hand in hand with realism. And fear darkens the outlook of the victors.

Wistfully we look back at the eighteenth-century man climbing his mountain slope, looking down on the ground fog of superstition and thrilled with the triumphs that reason had already achieved and the vision of others to come. It is worth recording that the man of the middle-years of the twentieth century has also passed through the fog—the fog of wartime confusion and uncertainties. He has emerged into the clear, hard light of an unlovely day. He has used reason to achieve triumphs of technology and of organization and finally to unlock the elemental energy of the cosmos. He has overthrown the high priests of the worship of naked power and has lifted the burden of militarism from the backs of oppressed and exploited millions. He has begun the hard task of building a new order.

The age of the mid-twentieth century is close kin to that of the Enlightenment. It may, in fact, one day be called in retrospect the New Enlightenment. If our investments in technology and in scientific laboratories have evidential value, we, like the men of the eighteenth century, have put our faith in reason. If our wars of liberation have any meaning, we have put our faith in the reality and the validity of the rights of humanity. We know, as did the men of the eighteenth century, that we are making a new world. And we know far better than did the men of the Enlightenment the evils that must be constantly fought off if we are to make progress. What we do not have is the élan of the young Jefferson writing the Declaration of Independence or the young Washington leading the rebel armies in the fight for liberty. But I venture to suggest that we may have it tomorrow. We are still oppressed with the weariness of years of war. But we are on the threshold of an age whose possibilities for advance are beyond the imagination. I have faith that the collective reason of the peoples of the world will be able to control and to harness for useful purposes the energy which science has loosed. In the midst of dynastic and imperial wars and of political and social revolutions, the eighteenth-century man held fast to high hope. Can the man who has shared in the prodigious triumphs of the middle years of the twentieth century do less? We are well advanced up the mountain slope. The fatiguing and dangerous trail ahead beckons us!

5

Evangelical Religion and Popular Romanticism in Early Nineteenth-Century America

Arnold Toynbee has described our Western civilization in the twentieth century as a rationalistic and secular culture. In the sense that an awareness of the importance of science is the starting point of the thinking of our day, the generalization seems true. We prize

SOURCE: This paper was read in the session on Church History at the American Historical Association meeting in Boston in December 1949, and was published in *Church History* 19, No. 1 (March 1950): 34-47. Reprinted with permission of The American Society of Church History.

the realism of the objective, analytical approach of science. In a turbulent and swiftly moving age we have substituted relativism for older values once confidently assumed to have universal validity. We have seen skepticism, born of twentieth-century events, erode an old and dynamic belief in progress. We observe Protestantism, its old orthodoxy shaken, striving to make the Christian tradition meaningful and significant for a materialistic generation. We watch the protagonists of democracy striving to hold fast to essential human values and to protect basic freedoms in an age of fear and power.

The twentieth-century man looks back with a certain wistfulness upon his forerunner in the eighteenth. Newton's mechanistic cosmos, symbolized by the ordered swinging of the planets about the sun, provided the starting point of eighteenth-century thought. The concept of the order of nature was central to the climate of opinion of eighteenth-century England and France, the provinces of the British crown in North America. The order of nature expressed itself in eighteenth-century America in a stable society of aristocrats and commoners, a society that in America produced leadership of sufficient quality to carry out a successful war of independence and to create an enduring Federal Republic. The order of nature, called into being by nature's God, to use Jefferson's phrase, emphasized the virtues of restraint and balance, the importance of reason, and the fundamental character of natural law. Washington expressed its norms in his self-restraint, after Yorktown, in the use of the vast personal power that came to him with victory. The eighteenth century prized realism and decorum. Its mood and values fitted well the life of small ordered communities east of the Appalachians, conscious of their past and confident of the future. In these communities Protestantism had lost much of the drive and power it had had in seventeenth-century New England. Even that restored by the Great Awakening had declined in the Revolutionary years. A deistic humanism provided the philosophy of the upper classes and had, through Tom Paine's

Appeal to Reason, a wide influence among common men.

Between the rationalism and the realism of the eighteenth century and that of the twentieth lies the period dealt with in the present inquiry. The first half of the nineteenth century saw the decline of Deism, the rise of evangelical Protestantism, and the final formulation of that cluster of ideas and values that made up the American democratic credo. The American Revolution, though the achievement of eighteenth-century men and the product of eighteenth-century thought, looked forward to the nineteenth. The Declaration of Independence, with its emphasis on liberty and its doctrine of equality, was to be accepted by later generations as the classic formulation of democratic theory. Before he went to France as minister of the United States, Jefferson wrote the Virginia statute of religious liberty, a liberty guaranteed and extended by the first amendment to the Federal Constitution. In America, the eighteenth century ended in the triumph of freedom. The men of that age, in harmony with their predilection for balance, linked freedom and responsibility. They had won freedom both for the political state and for religion; they made both the state and religion the responsibility of the people.

In Western Europe the French Revolution separated the nineteenth from the eighteenth century. In the United States the surmounting of the Appalachian barrier and the establishment of a fluid and rapidly moving frontier west of the mountains marked the boundary between the two epochs. In the first half of the nineteenth century, Americans streamed westward. They filed through the passes of the Alleghenies on horseback and in Conestoga wagons. They took the leisurely boat passage on the Erie Canal. They moved westward singly, in families, and by companies. They subdued to cultivated fields the rich soils of the Ohio and Mississippi valleys. Refusing to be balked by dry plains, mountains, or deserts, they pushed on to the shores of the Pacific, where they supplanted the descendants of the Spanish conquerors. Moreover, as covered wagons jolted toward the Pacific, other

Americans harnessed Atlantic streams to new machines in new factories that multiplied in size and number with each passing decade. "It was our first great period of exploitation," remarked Vernon Parrington, writing beside Puget Sound in 1927, "and from it emerged, as naturally as the cock from the mother egg, the spirit of romance, gross and tawdry in vulgar minds, dainty and refined in the more cultivated. But always romance. The days of realism were past, and it was quietly laid away with the wig and the smallclothes of an outworn generation."[1] The nineteenth-century frontier, subliterate, undisciplined, and materialistic, tested the ability of the common people of the United States to measure up to the responsibility, placed upon them by religious freedom, to preserve that ancient Christian tradition that had come to America from Europe.

Timothy Dwight, leader of Connecticut Congregationalism and president of Yale College, journeyed about the turn of the century to the back country to observe at first hand the ways of the frontiersmen. "The business of these men," he wrote in 1810, in a passage destined to become famous, "is no other than to cut down trees, build log-houses, lay open forested ground to cultivation, and prepare the way for those who come after them. These men cannot live in regular society. They are too idle, too talkative, too passionate, too prodigal, and too shiftless to acquire either property or character. They are impatient of law, religion, and morality. . . . At the same time they are possessed, in their own view, of uncommon wisdom; understand medical science, politics, and religion better than those who have studied them through life; and, although they manage their own concerns worse than any other men, feel perfectly satisfied that they can manage those of the nation far better than the agents to whom they are committed by the public." Dwight, austere gentleman of the tie-wig school, found the rough folk of the frontier log cabins and stump lots given to passion and to exaggeration in talk and behavior. An oral literature of tall tales about those mythical heroes, Mike Fink, Davy Crockett, and Paul Bunyan, enlivened social gatherings from the Great Lakes forests to those of the Gulf coast. These extravagant and earthy narratives of the bunkhouse, the flatboat, and the tap room glorified the individual. Davy Crockett became a cosmic figure who twisted the tails of comets as well as catamounts. These Brobdingnagian yarns, whose humor lacked any discipline of wit, reflected a society in which ability and readiness to use one's fists was frequently the primary factor in determining the status of the individual. Dwight's staid Connecticut had no counterpart for the frontier gouging fight where no holds were barred. Dwight inevitably looked with a jaundiced eye upon the unkempt population of the frontier. What he did not realize was that the future lay with that rowdy, illiterate, yet fundamentally creative, frontier.

Unlike Connecticut, where the separation of church and state was not finally effected until 1818, religion on the frontier became from the beginning the full responsibility of the common people organized into voluntary congregations. The people of the back country, selecting what they could understand of the Christian tradition, turned that tradition to their own purposes. They transformed those meager elements of Western civilization that trans-Appalachian migrants brought from eastern communities into folk culture. North of the Ohio this culture was a short transitional phase in the evolution of civilization. South of that river, due in part to the tardy emergence of public schools, a folk culture persisted for generations. In this western country evangelical Protestantism became a folk religion, expressing the attitudes of the people and providing for their intellectual and emotional needs. Among a population whose principal literature was the remembered tale, the Bible became the one important book. Its narrative gave to this culture its historical perspective. The precepts and admonitions of the Old and New Testaments established authoritative norms for the governing of human conduct, norms that were nothing less than the fixed and eternal laws of God established for the ordering of society. But, though the Bible spoke with authority, its words had to be interpreted, and no established church provided a single authoritative interpretation. Herein lay the essence of that religious liberty which had been guaranteed by the First Amendment to the Constitution. Among this frontier population existed many individual minds of great native capacity, but they were walled-in by ignorance and isolated from the world of thought by the lack of educational opportunity. Such minds, making use of the only intellectual materials at hand, acquired, many times, a prodigious biblical learning and even advanced to a homespun variety of philosophical and theological speculation. These individuals, often becoming leaders of local groups, played an important part in that splintering of Protestantism that was so pronounced a phenomenon of the nineteenth century.

The extravagance and individualism of the tall tales appeared again in the emotional experiences of the converted sinners of the frontier camp meetings. Back country folk invented this form of religious association and in it created not only a pattern for public worship but a means of expressing those emotions so fundamental to human life. Emotions are called up out of the depths of human nature by conflict and by rhythm. Evangelical Protestantism provided both. It presented the drama of the conflict of the Lord with the Devil for mastery in a world of sinners. It managed its greatest climax in the conflict of the individual sinner with his sin. The hysterical phenomena associated with the revival type of conversion are one of the commonplaces of frontier history. Unlettered exhorters preached what they understood to be the Christian message to country folk assembled from widely scattered cabins. In clearings lighted by flickering campfires, the preaching continued far into the night. The religious song, however, more than the spoken word, moved the mourner to grief for his sin and exaltation at his escape therefrom. The white spirituals, like the tall tales, were the creation of the folk culture of the back country. In these spirituals evangelical Protestantism, as a folk religion, came to focus.

These songs evolved out of older materials carried to the frontier by emigrants from eastern communities. Eighteenth-century Methodist and Baptist hymns underwent transformation. An unknown author of the time of Wesley wrote the stately hymn that ran:

> A few more days on earth to spend
> And all my toils and cares shall end,
> And I shall see my God and friend
> And praise his name on high.

Transformed by frontier influences, the stanza emerged as a refrain in the vernacular of the back settlements for a swiftly moving camp meeting revival song:

> I pitch my tent on this camp ground,
>   Few days, few days!
> And give old Satan another round,
>   And I am going home.
> I can't stay in these diggings,
>   Few days, few days!
> I can't stay in these diggings,
>   I am going home.

Other white spirituals were modifications of popular songs of the day. Many were sad and mournful songs dealing with farewell and death and set in a minor key. Through practically all ran a rhythm that lent itself to handclapping, stamping, and marching. Back country worshippers called the clapping, swaying accompaniment "the shout." The shout reinforced the emotional experience derived from these songs and from the worship of which they were a part. Ecstasy was the end sought, the supreme good, a good that could be enjoyed in the here and now. The men and women of the settlements were proud of the shout; they sang about it. Referring to the Judgment Day in one song, the swaying, clapping mourners chanted:

> Sweet morning, sweet morning
> And we'll all shout together
> In the morning.

They thought of Heaven as a place where the shout continued. In these spirituals of evangelical Protestantism, untutored men and women could forget for a moment the drabness and squalor, the pains and sorrows, of poor and isolated communities in a dazzling, romantic vision of pearly gates and golden streets. People whose place was near the bottom of the social hierarchy of the age sang of personal triumph and glory in the spirit of the aggressive individualism of the frontier.

> I want to see bright angels stand
> And waiting to receive me.[2]

The folk religion of the exuberant, optimistic, and undisciplined frontier represented a bizarre, but nonetheless genuine, expression of the spirit of romanticism. This religion had power. It helped to subdue the grosser evils of the frontier. It made an impress on American society that persisted far into the twentieth century.

New England in the first half of the nineteenth century looked at frontier society with apprehension and with a fear that expressed itself politically in the Hartford convention at the end of the War of 1812. New England, moreover, deeply resented the condescending generalizations of such foreign visitors as Mrs. Trollope who insisted that frontier uncouthness provided the true picture of American character. "There is no literary atmosphere breathing through the forests or across the prairies," declared Horace Bushnell as late as 1847. This Congregational clergyman and theologian of Hartford, Connecticut, had before this date challenged the conservatism of his New England colleagues. He had, in fact, become a prophet who was pointing out a new way that was ultimately to lead to the social gospel of the latter years of the century. In 1847, however, Bushnell was not immediately concerned with theology. He was stumping the East from New York to Boston in the cause of home missions. He chose for the title of his address, "Barbarism the First Danger." Affirming that frontier colleges, "if they have any, are only rudimental beginnings, and the youth a raw company of woodsmen," he solicited money to rescue westerners from the darkness of ignorance and sin. "Be it also understood," he concluded in a peroration that mirrored a blend of New England practicality and complacency, "that the sooner we have railroads and telegraphs spinning into the wilderness, and setting the remotest hamlets in connection and close proximity with the east, the more certain it is that light, good manners and Christian refinement will become universally diffused. For when the emigrant settlements of Minnesota or of Oregon feel that they are just in the suburb of Boston, it is nearly the same thing, in fact, as if they actually were."[3] The tendency of Europeans to see American culture in terms of western "barbarism" spurred eastern men of letters to attempt to create what was, in effect, a derivative culture. Longfellow, the translator, was the most important in this group. Emerson, however, refused to follow the intellectual fashions of his day. He rejected sterile imitation. He would have no truck with a culture that "fed on the sere remains of foreign harvests."[4]

Emerson and the Concord transcendentalists stood at the opposite pole of intellectual sophistication from contemporary camp meeting exhorters and from the creators of the white spirituals. Transcendentalism, together with the folk religion of the frontier, enables us to set early nineteenth-century Protestantism in perspective. In New England a liberal movement called Unitarianism in the first half of the century tried to modify an older Puritanism, to reconcile theology with Newtonian science, and to subdue to reason the thorny doctrine of the Trinity. Emerson began his adult career as a Unitarian preacher. When he became convinced that the new liberalism had become little more than the urbane philosophy of upper class respectability, he walked out of the pulpit. Emerson sympathized with the ethical emphasis of Unitarianism, for he, together with the colleagues of William Ellery Channing, inherited the ethical seriousness of seventeenth-century Puritanism. But in Emerson's eyes Unitarianism had lost its drive; its ethic had declined into a cult of respectability. For Emerson, Unitarianism was like the conch shell he picked up on the sand and in which, when he held it to his ear, he could hear only the distant echo of the sea. He craved an immediate experience of the crash of the breakers on the shore. As he moved away from Unitarian rationalism, Emerson, however, did not take the road to orthodoxy. His trail led, rather, in the opposite direction toward what his outraged Protestant contemporaries called the new infidelity. Ethics remained his preoccupation; he sought a faith that would be a dynamism giving ethics significance in society. The discovery by Emerson and Thoreau of nature as a source of inspiration is one of the most familiar of American stories. Nature brought them into contact with that infinite and immanent God that these transcendentalists called the Over-Soul. Through mystical experience Emerson discovered what William James, in a later generation, described as "that peace abiding at the heart of endless agitation." Emerson's lines to the tiny purple Rhodora, blooming in solitude, express better than almost any other among his writings the transcendentalist mood and the transcendentalist affirmation of the unity of nature, man, and God.

Why thou wert there, O rival of the rose
I never thought to ask, I never knew:
But, in my simple ignorance, suppose
The self-same Power that brought me there brought you.

Mystical experience convinced Emerson that deity dwells in the human heart, a belief that led to his conviction that the individual man has vast potential powers, that every man has a unique mission in the world, a contribution that he alone can make and which the world needs. Emerson's definition of individualism as uniqueness and nonconformity surpassed even that of the frontier.

Between New England transcendentalism and the folk religion of the frontier ran the main current of American Protestantism in an age in which cities were growing swiftly but whose outlook was still dominated by that of the countryside and the rural village. As the century rolled forward, New England theology lost some of that granite hardness of Puritan Calvinism and took on the adaptable rationality of Scottish common sense. Jonathan Edwards in the eighteenth century, moreover, had introduced the idea of the importance of emotion into what had been a coldly logical intellectual structure. Emotion had made its way in the churches despite a somewhat stubborn conservatism of theologians. The significance of religious feeling ultimately found its greatest exponent in Horace Bushnell. As "the ideal of Greeks was beauty," he remarked in 1843, "and that of the Romans law, so this new age shall embrace an ideal more comprehensive, as it is higher than all, namely love. . . . This love is no partial ideal, as every other must be; it is universal, it embraces all that is beneficent, pure, true, beautiful—God, man, eternity, time." In such an outlook and philosophy the social gospel was born. Bushnell also, like Emerson, had his moments of emotional exaltation. Early in December 1852, returning from the West, the Hartford preacher paused to look at Niagara Falls. His was the familiar pilgrimage of the early nineteenth-century Americans to the natural wonder. Thousands who could not make the journey knew the Falls through published engravings made from the romantic canvases of the landscapists of the Hudson River school. "I was never so deeply impressed with them before," commented Bushnell in a letter he posted to his wife, ". . . one ocean plunging in solemn repose of continuity into another . . . a power that is the same yesterday, today, and forever. . . I could hardly stand, such was the sense it gave me of the greatness of God. . . .''[5] Though Bushnell attacked the nature worship of the transcendentalists six years later in a volume he called *Nature and the Supernatural*, his thought, in spite of the fact that he used the phrases of the familiar Protestant orthodoxy, disclosed close kinship to that of Emerson. Both men found nature the source of inspiration, and both looked upon man as the culmination of nature. Both exalted the individual and emphasized the importance of the free expression of his emotions. At this point it is useful to recall that early nineteenth-century romanticism emphasized just these things—the importance of nature as a manifestation of beauty and a source of inspiration, the value of the individual, and the significance of the emotions of men. Whatever their intellectual differences, Bushnell and Emerson both belonged to that international company of romantics so important in the early nineteenth-century world.

Looking backward from our day we can see that Bushnell was primarily important for the second half of the nineteenth century, as his thought led out into the social gospel. A much simpler man than he pioneered in eastern communities in the development of emotional expression in early nineteenth-century Protestantism. Lowell Mason, hymn-writer, emerged in a period in which all of the United States, with unimportant exceptions, was little better than a musical wilderness. His greatest secular achievement came when he persuaded the educational authorities of Boston to lead the nation in putting musical instruction into the schools of that city. The state of early nineteenth-century American music is suggested by the fact that as late as 1837, the year of Emerson's Phi Beta Kappa address at Harvard, Mason's *New Collection of Church Music* devoted twenty-four opening pages to instruction in the ''elements of vocal music.'' Mason did not merely collect and make available the religious songs of Europe and older America. He became the most important American creator of hymns of the first half of the nineteenth century. While he still lived, his songs became the household possessions of millions of his fellow countrymen. There were few Americans who did not know "My Faith Looks Up to Thee," "From Greenland's Icy Mountains," or "Nearer My God to Thee." They became what Mason intended them to be, songs of the people. He combined simple poems of aspiration with melodies that were equally simple. He rose on occasion to moderate heights of emotional expression and at times declined into sentimentality. Toward the end of his life, Mason set down the philosophy that governed him in the creation of those songs that moved the men and women of his day. Congregational singing, he remarked in 1859, "is nature's method of praise. It is, in a great degree independent of art culture, being indeed above art. It is adapted alike to the voices of the young and the old, the uncultivated and the cultivated. It engages all in the simultaneous exercise of the same emotions. . . . It belongs . . . to the sublime in nature rather than in art. It may be compared to the mountains, which owe their majesty, not to their fertile soil, nor to any architectural skill, but to the Power which commanded the light to shine out of darkness, and brought up from the depths the rough and diversified materials in which consists 'the strength of the hills.' " The character of this affirmation and the choice of metaphor make clear that Mason selected his word, nature, from the vocabulary of mid-nineteenth-century romanticism. Mason was as much affected by the romantic spirit as Bushnell or Emerson. What the white spirituals contributed to the folk religion of the frontier Mason's hymns gave to the worship of the churches of more developed communities. When the folk culture of the early settlements gave way before the advance of civilization, Mason's hymns replaced the spirituals. With their frank appeal to emotion, these songs of the people played a part in softening the craggy theology of older New England and in preparing the way for Bushnell's manifesto concerning the law of love.

"Upon close inspection," commented Alexis de Tocqueville as

he surveyed the society of early nineteenth-century America, "it will be seen that there is in every age some peculiar and preponderant fact with which all others are connected; this fact almost always gives birth to some pregnant idea or some ruling passion, which attracts to itself and bears away in its course all the feelings and opinions of the time; it is like a great stream toward which each of the neighboring rivulets seems to flow."[6] Tocqueville seems to have thought that individualism, born of freedom in the American environment, was such a ruling idea. "*Individualism*," he noted, "is a novel expression to which a novel idea has given birth."[7] Early nineteenth-century Protestantism, whether that of frontier folk religion or that of the more sophisticated denominations, focused on the individual, as did also New England transcendentalism. Both Protestantism and transcendentalism, moreover, emphasized the importance of the emotions of the individual man and woman. Though the ecstasy of frontier revivalistic religious experience has been labeled a manifestation of sect tradition and practices while such communion with nature as that of Bushnell and Emerson has been called mysticism, the similarities between the two types of individual emotional experience outweigh the differences. Nineteenth-century Protestantism as a people's religion and transcendentalism as a faith for the more cultivated few were both, at bottom, romantic religions. Though such influences cannot be measured, it is a reasonable guess that Christianity had as much to do with giving romanticism its dominant position in the climate of opinion of mid-nineteenth-century America as did literary and artistic importations from across the Atlantic.

As Tocqueville suggested, there is an alchemy at work in every climate of opinion that tends to dissolve inconsistencies and to establish fundamental agreements. The concept of the order of nature was such an agent in the eighteenth century. In the first half of the nineteenth century, romanticism provided the solvent. It permeated the arts and literature. It expressed itself in the South in the cult of chivalry and in the romantic nationalism of the dream of the Confederate States of America. It created the fundamental similarities between religious and secular thinking. The eighteenth century had bequeathed to the common man of the nineteenth responsibility for organized religion on the one hand and for the political state on the other. Inevitably, the citizen expressed similar ideas as his thinking moved back and forth between these two realms.

The first half of the nineteenth century, as Parrington affirmed, was a time of conquest and of exploitation. As the decades advanced, Americans achieved a deepening understanding of the nature and significance of the evils that were poisoning their society—unintelligent and often cruel treatment of the mentally ill, urban slums that grew more rapidly than the cities, chattel slavery whose continuous existence mocked the pretensions of democracy. A somber realism appeared, expressing itself in the early writings of Parke Goodwin of New York City and in the hardhitting sermons of Theodore Parker in Boston. The realism, however, was not well done by twentieth-century standards of social science, for early nineteenth-century Americans still lived in what was, in reality, a pre-scientific age. The two greatest tracts of a golden age of tracts, *Uncle Tom's Cabin* and *Ten Nights in a Barroom*, fell short of achieving even literary realism. Their vast success in their own time lay not in an artistic recreation of human life distorted by social evils but rather in the fact that they frankly laid siege to the emotions of a generation brought up on the emotionalism of evangelical Protestantism. Romanticism emphasized the nobility of feelings of concern for suffering humanity. In the varied humanitarian movements that grew to significance in early nineteenth-century America, a generous sympathy for the less favored, the unfortunate, and the oppressed made up for inadequate knowledge of society and of the forces that move within it. In spite of inadequacies in scientific knowledge, however, the drive toward betterment of society and the realization of democratic ideals brought concrete results—universal manhood suffrage in Jackson's day, establishment on a sure foundation of the public school system, and abandonment of the legal theory of the English common law that labor unions are conspiracies. Romantic emotionalism had power in humanitarian undertakings as well as in religion.

Above the humanitarian crusades and the concrete social advances, a cluster of democratic norms emerged that Whitman, before he became the poet of American democracy, called the American faith.[8] It was a credo announced on every ceremonial national occasion from public platforms. It inspired a literature that ran the gamut from Bancroft's history to Whitman's "Leaves of Grass." Although the statements of the pattern of democratic idealism were only seldom couched in the analytical vocabulary of logic, they have been broken down into specific doctrines. The primary doctrine was that of the fundamental law not made by man underlying society and making human association possible, the natural law of the Declaration of Independence and the moral law of Christian tradition. The emphasis was on permanence in the time and universal validity among men. The second doctrine was that of the free and responsible individual, responsible not only for contributing to the management of the political state but ultimately to the fundamental law before which all men are equal. This doctrine was the secular counterpart of the religious affirmation of the ultimate responsibility of the individual to God. In the same first half of the nineteenth century, when American Protestants moved outward to establish mission stations on the frontier and in non-Christian lands, the doctrine of a national mission to stand before the world as a witness for democracy came into being. The parallels between this early nineteenth-century democratic faith and the romantic Christianity of the people seem clear. To the similarities in ideas must be added similarities in emotional emphasis. "Not in an obscure corner, not in feudal Europe . . ." said Emerson, voicing the hope that democracy would one day bring peace to the world, "is this seed of benevolence laid in the furrow

with tears of hope, but in the broad America of God and man.''
The democratic credo was also a romantic formulation. It came
to focus in its concept of the dignity of the individual—a concept
which had also been central to the rationalistic and generous
humanism of the eighteenth-century Enlightenment. In the
nineteenth century, though experience and logic provided important reinforcement, the essential dynamism of this doctrine of the
dignity of man, when it expressed itself in humanitarian undertakings, was not reason but rather emotion born of desire and faith.
This democratic credo, this American dream, was the greatest
achievement of an age that, in retrospect, we see as but an interlude
between two periods of rationalism and realism, an age, moreover,
that came to an end when mid-nineteenth-century Americans
abandoned rational debate and, surrendering to their hates and
fears, marched off to fratricidal war.

Notes

[1]Vernon Parrington, *Main Currents of American Thought*, II, p. v.
[2]George P. Jackson, *White Sprituals in the Southern Uplands* (Chapel
Hill, N.C., 1933) p. 298, 302.
[3]Horace Bushnell, *Barbarism the First Danger* (New York, 1947), p.
6, 27.
[4]*American Scholar*.
[5]Mary A. (Bushnell) Cheney, ed., *Life and Letters* (New York, 1880),
p. 276-277.
[6]Alexis de Tocqueville, *Democracy in America*, Phillips Bradley ed.,
II (New York, 1945), p. 95.
[7]Ibid., p. 98.
[8]Ralph H. Gabriel, *The Course of American Democratic Thought*
(New York, 1940), p. 12-25.

6

Thomas Jefferson and Twentieth-Century Rationalism

One evening in 1944 I dined in Washington with a counsellor of the Polish embassy, a representative of the Polish government in exile. I had come up from the War Department School of Military Government at Charlottesville, Virginia, where I had known well some Polish officers, friends of my embassy host. As we talked at dinner, the Polish representative told me that the place in Washington he liked best to visit was the Jefferson Memorial. He preferred it to the Washington home at Mount Vernon, the Lee Shrine at Arlington, or even the Lincoln Memorial. The Jefferson Memorial was then scarcely a year old. In the spring of 1943 the President of the United States had joined with other national leaders in dedicating the modified replica of the Pantheon done in white marble in

SOURCE: Reprinted, with permission, from *The Virginia Quarterly Review* 26, No. 3 (Summer 1950): 321-335.

the center of which rises the tall, silent figure of Thomas Jefferson. Set in bronze on the walls are words that Jefferson wrote not only on paper but in his life. My host told me that he never let pass an opportunity to take his friends, particularly his European friends, to the memorial.

The new importance of Jefferson was not without its surprising aspect. Americans of the first half of the nineteenth century elevated Washington to the position of the supreme national folk hero. The generation that followed Appomattox put Lincoln beside the eighteenth-century leader. A mere glance, however, at the map of the United States reveals the nineteenth-century evaluation of Jefferson. His name is seldom found as an American place name. When Colorado entered the Union in 1876, the centennial year of the Declaration of Independence, Congress refused the request of the men of that frontier that the new state be called Jefferson. Through nearly a century and a half of national history Jefferson was remembered as a political figure, his name bracketed with that of Hamilton, as the name of the rising Lincoln in the late 1850s was bracketed with that of Douglas. Lincoln transcended the association before his martyrdom and, surpassing even Washington, emerged in the twentieth century as the most beloved and most powerful of American hero symbols. No American can stand before the seated figure in the temple beside the Potomac without an emotional experience akin to that of religion. Then in the late 1930s a subtle alchemy working in American culture caused the name of Jefferson to transcend that of Hamilton, until the planter of Monticello took his place in American tradition beside the master of Mount Vernon and the lawyer of Springfield. The evidence for the change may be found in increasing references to Jefferson in the literature of the discussion of democracy. A growing and impressive list of biographies and biographical studies began to recreate for a twentieth-century generation this eighteenth-century man, not merely as a political figure but as a farmer, an architect, and a philosopher. Then the United States built the memorial beside the Potomac, using with fine taste the Rotunda which Jefferson designed at the University of Virginia as the inspiration. The magnification of Jefferson culminated in the decision to recover and to publish every word that Jefferson wrote. The first volume of this Brobdingnagian undertaking has already gone into type. The counsellor of the Polish embassy conducting his European friends to the memorial to look at the serene figure and to read the words set on the walls took the shrine for granted. To the student of American thought, however, this recent and belated episode in the history of American tradition contained so many elements of paradox as to suggest inquiry into its meaning.

A cursory glance at mid-twentieth-century America discloses some of the paradoxes. Jefferson was a farmer who feared the city mechanic and who maintained that the independent husbandman was and must continue to be the principal supporter and carrier of the American democratic tradition. The generation that built the memorial had been shaped by an industrial and urban revolution that had multiplied the number of city mechanics until they had become a vast company exercising great political power and had reduced the farmers to a minority among American economic groups. Jefferson emphasized the individual as against the government. He insisted that the government is best that governs least and that democracy is most effectively practiced in local as opposed to centralized national government. The generation that built the memorial had put its faith not only in big government but in centralized national government. Moreover, the events that have followed the close of World War II have made clear that this shift must be considered a permanent rather than a transitory change in American thinking.

But the paradox of the emergence of Jefferson as a major folk hero in the middle of the twentieth century has subtler aspects associated with what Joseph Wood Krutch, literary and dramatic critic, called in 1929 the "modern temper" and Jerome Frank, New York lawyer and later federal judge, spoke of in 1930 as the "modern mind." The nineteenth century ended in 1914 when Europe collapsed into war. The twentieth century began in America with a change of mind. Krutch ran his eye swiftly over the long span between the ancient world of Greece and Rome and that of 1929. "Races," he remarked, "as well as individuals have their infancy, their adolescence, and their maturity. . . . As civilization grows older, it . . . has more and more facts thrust upon its consciousness and is compelled to abandon one after another, quite as a child does, certain illusions that have been dear to it." Krutch thought science had created the modern outlook. Science, particularly Darwin's biology, Freud's psychology, and Einstein's theory of relativity, had compelled the modern man to give up the old and comforting dream world of poetry, mythology, and religion. Poetry, mythology, and religion, thought Krutch, are formulae for security. Krutch, and later Frank, insisted that we live in a changing world. "The modern mind," Frank added, "is a mind free of childish emotional drags, a mature mind. There develops a sort of 'adult agnosticism.' "

II

The eighteenth century shaped the mind of Thomas Jefferson. The men of that age, impressed by the harmony and the grandeur of Newton's mechanistic universe, disclosed by reason, put aside superstition as they understood it and in their day moved forward in the light of science. They called theirs the Age of Enlightenment. Watching the planets swing silently and majestically about the sun, they saw order in the created universe and made the concept of the order of nature central to their world outlook. Eighteenth-century thinking emphasized a new plateau to which man had climbed. Newton's triumph in discovering the mechanics that control the starry night had stimulated the imaginations of the somewhat formal generation that came after him to a point where the men of the eighteenth century became convinced that reason could penetrate to the ultimate secrets of the Author of Nature. Man, possessed of reason, had dignity, even, in Newton's case, majesty. Reason had brought progress in knowledge; it could also bring progress in human nature. Out of the concepts of the dignity of man and of his capacity for improvement came the insight that the inevitable corollary of human dignity is freedom. Jefferson assumed, as the common sense of the subject, that because man is a part of nature liberty must also be inherent in nature. The young representative from Virginia in the Continental Congress made natural rights the central theme of the Declaration of Independence. Jefferson assumed with his eighteenth-century contemporaries that, if reason was universal among mankind, the natural right to achieve dignity through liberated reason was also universal. The doctrine provided the foundation for a generous and hopeful humanism.

The nineteenth century had many reasons that need not be considered here for declining to think of Jefferson as any more important than a number of other actors in the stirring scenes attendant upon the founding of the nation. But the doctrine of natural rights and the idea of moral values of universal validity persisted. They found expression in the early twentieth century in the dynamic idealism of Woodrow Wilson in World War I. Before Wilson coined his famous phrases, however, the emergence in the late nineteenth century of a new skepticism suggested that Americans might be changing their minds. Charles Darwin had altered and deepened men's understanding of nature. William Graham Sumner, forthright and hardhitting lecturer and publicist, led the attack upon eighteenth-century doctrine. Darwin's nature, he growled, gives man no right even to life, let alone liberty. Nature merely gives man a chance to live—if he can. "It is an easy way to attain the objects of our desire," he added contemptuously, "to put them in the list of the 'rights of man' or to resolve that 'we are and of right ought to be' what we would like to be."

Mr. Justice Holmes, with that urbanity and charm that endeared him to his generation, took up the same theme in 1918. ''There is in all men a demand for the superlative,'' he remarked, ''so much so that the poor devil who has no other way of reaching it attains it by getting drunk. It seems to me that this demand is at the bottom of the philosopher's efforts to prove that truth is absolute and of the jurist's search for criteria of universal validity which he collects under the head of natural law. . . . The jurists who believe in natural law seem to me to be in that naive state of mind that accepts what has been accepted by them and their neighbors as something that must be accepted by men everywhere.'' Holmes became the prophet of a significant company of avant-garde legal thinkers that became important in the law schools and on the bench. For Holmes and the new school of legal realists, the law had ceased to be an abstract entity present as the foundation of order in nature or even as the meaning of the statute to be found by the judge. Law is the product of experience in a changing world. The judge in deciding between the disputants in a case before him makes the law. The Constitution, Charles Evans Hughes once remarked, is what the Supreme Court says it is. ''If the people are not in command of their own government,'' added Federal Judge Charles E. Clark in 1942, ''but are actually subordinate to some remote sovereign who upholds and justifies unsanitary conditions, poor housing, long hours of labor, and general defiance of social welfare as a freedom required by some vague constitutional command or higher law of nature, then we are nearer either anarchy or the rule of the autocratic few than we are democracy.'' The legal realism of Holmes and Clark suggests Jerome Frank's meaning when he insisted that a prime characteristic of the modern mind is ''adult agnosticism.''

Agnosticism went further. The eighteenth-century man had taken it for granted that basic moral values have universal validity. Holmes, the hero of the American liberals of the 1930s, doubted universality. ''I loathe war,'' he wrote in 1920 to his old friend Sir Frederick Pollock, ''but I do think that man at present is a predatory animal. I think that the sacredness of human life is a purely municipal ideal of no validity outside the jurisdiction.'' Outside the jurisdiction—here is the concept of relativity in the area of ethical ideas. The norm that expresses a good for one jurisdiction does not necessarily carry weight in another. Holmes phrased in the language of the law a conclusion of the anthropologists of the mid-twentieth century. Returning from their field trips to the subliterate cultures of the Pacific Islands, of Africa, and of the Western Hemisphere, these students of the ways of man pointed out that each culture they had investigated had its own values, its own ethical norms. Holmes translated this ethical relativism into words that every man could understand. "I don't believe," the Justice wrote in 1926 to a young Chinese friend and admirer, "that it is an absolute principle or even a human ultimate that man always is an end in himself—that his dignity must be respected, etc. . . . Our morality seems to me only a check on the ultimate domination of force, just as our politeness is a check on the impulse of every pig to put his feet in the trough. When the Germans in the late war disregarded [in their use of the submarine] what we called the rules of the game, I don't see that there was anything to be said except: we don't like it and shall kill you if we can.'' Holmes carried his realism from law into ethics. If logic brought him to unpleasant conclusions, he refused to conceal them under a gloss of hypocrisy.

There is a strain toward consistency in the thought of a period. The emphasis in the 1920s and 1930s upon particular ethical systems in particular cultures had its counterpart in political thought in the emphasis on nationalism. Ethical relativity as between cultures, moreover, in effect denied a morality existing to control the relations among nations. The so-called science of geopolitics that emerged into prominence after World War I insisted that nation-states are in the last analysis power structures and that power is the ultimate arbiter in the international world. Intellectuals, pursuing the new realism in matters international, began to speak persuasively in the 1930s of the never-ending power struggle among the nations. Nicholas Spykman in that decade declared to large classes of Yale undergraduates and to an international audience in a widely read book that the world had come into a time not only of total war but of continuous war. The so-called periods of peace, he insisted, are merely times when economic and political conflict replace the struggle of arms and when wise nations make preparations for the next test of armed strength. The realism of geopolitics with its preoccupation with a Darwinian intertribal struggle was part of a twentieth-century naturalistic rationalism that emphasized particularity.

The strain toward consistency, moreover, brought emphasis on particularity in a place where it was to be least expected. Liberal American Protestantism had supported World War I as a war to end war and a crusade to make the world safe for democracy. After 1918 many Protestant leaders, disillusioned by the failure of the peace and chastened by their too easy acceptance of the propaganda of the warring powers, followed the brilliant and consecrated Harry Emerson Fosdick into the support of pacifism as the Christian answer to the doctrine of power of geopolitics. The change marked a swing in Protestant circles from the extreme of what had been almost a holy war to the opposite extreme of passive resistance. Gandhi of India became a prophet not only for his own people but for the American Fellowship of Reconciliation. Proclaiming war as the most monstrous of evils, many leaders of the pacifist group urged upon the United States a policy of isolation to keep American citizens free from entanglement in the tribal conflicts of Europe. Even the road of high idealism led to particularity.

I attempt no complete canvass of the naturalistic rationalism of the period between the wars. The positions of the would-be science of geopolitics contained a considerable measure of demonstrable truth as the present Cold War makes amply clear. In those interbellum years science, because of its triumphs in technology and in medicine, had, in general, a vast prestige. The word "scientific" became one of the most potent adjectives in the American language and as such was appropriated by hopeful vendors of all sorts whose goods ranged from cigarettes that did not irritate the throat to Marxism which promised a classless utopia. In such an age, when ethics was looked upon as a system limited to the jurisdiction and when the jurisdiction was a nation engaged in a perpetual power struggle with its contemporaries, the older idealism of the nineteenth century seemed remote and unreal. Some thought of ideals as in the category of decoration like jewels, aesthetically beautiful but of little significance in a rough-and-tumble real world. Lincoln Steffens returned from a long sojourn in Europe in the late 1920s to write the autobiography of a disillusioned muck-raker who now saw the naiveté of the idealism behind the indignant pieces he once had written about corruption in the cities. At this point in his career Steffens went all out for pragmatism.

In the middle 1930s Thurman Arnold, legal realist, put ideals into the category of folklore. Then, taking a hint from the an-thropologists, Arnold emphasized the importance of folklore for the maintenance of national solidarity. "It was this faith in a higher law," remarked Arnold in 1937, "which made the Supreme Court the greatest unifying symbol of the American government. . . . To find peace men denounced government by men, and sought relief by reciting principles." Of course, this folklore was false. Such folklore must always be false, Arnold insisted, "in order to func-tion effectively" because folklore "must express contradictory ideals and must authoritatively suppress any facts which interfere with those ideals." Then James Burnham in the second of his three periods, on the threshold of the 1940s, mobilized the arguments of determinism to demonstrate that the American democratic dream was no more than a mirage and that the managerial revolution provided the authentic picture of the future. The list could be multiplied many times of those Americans who were convinced they had realism, to use a Darwinian metaphor, by the tail.

But even as Arnold and Burnham wrote, Jefferson was, at long last, stepping forward to take his place beside Washington and

Lincoln in the vanguard of American heroes. In the same year in which Burnham brought out *The Machiavellians*, the nation dedicated the marble memorial beside the Potomac and engraved on its walls those outmoded Jeffersonian phrases of the Declaration of Independence, which proclaimed the faith that men are created equal and that all men everywhere have certain inalienable natural rights. Did the ceremonies of April 13, 1943, merely open a new chapter in American folklore as interpreted by Thurman Arnold? Or did the event suggest that Americans were again changing their minds?

III

A partial answer to these questions may be found in certain dilemmas that confronted in the 1940s the realism of the years between the wars. According to Holmes and the rest of the significant company of legal realists, the judge, that is the official, makes the law. The year 1943 concluded a decade in which Americans had observed the progress of events in Germany where the Nazi hierarchy had not only preached but practiced the doctrine that the official makes the law. At the same time Americans who had insisted that relativism provides the only realistic approach to ethics discovered that a philosophy of ethical relativism made any American criticism of genocide as practiced by the Nazis within their jurisdiction irrelevant. If such practices were esteemed good in German culture, was it not an impertinence for Americans, who lived in a different culture, to object? The rediscovery of Jefferson, who believed that ethical principles of universal validity underlie society, suggests that the dedication of the new memorial in the national capital was more than an expression of the Arnold type of national folklore. The idea of fundamental human rights applicable to all men everywhere had begun to take form. Americans, moreover, had started to move toward the principle of universalism in world politics as well as ethics as they assisted significantly in the fabrication of the United Nations.

Then Hiroshima opened the door upon a new age—an age in which half a decade has seen the flaming terror in the sky grow to such magnitude as to transcend description by any earthly metaphor. The events of the same half decade, moreover, have seemed to bear out Spykman's grim analysis of total and perpetual war. The acceptance of the theory of the inevitability of the power struggle in the area of international relations helps to produce situations that verify the theory.

In the autumn of 1947 Edmund Sinnott, geneticist, member of the governing board of the Brookhaven Atomic Laboratory, and director of the Sheffield Scientific School, addressed an audience of the nation's most distinguished scientists assembled to celebrate the centennial of that institution. "Our world is out of joint," he said simply and with no effort at rhetoric.

> The crisis that confronts us is no ordinary one, but puts in peril not only our civilization but the very existence of our race on earth. This crisis has arisen from the fact that intellectual achievement, as expressed in the progress of the sciences, is cumulative and has been able to outrun the moral and esthetic qualities of man. . . . Man's control over the forces of the material world has grown to be far greater than his mastery of himself. No mere advance in intellectual power is going to meet this danger. No social mechanism, no economic system can save us now. To direct all science solely to the service of society, as some would have us do, will not suffice. Let us face the fact that what the world must have is a fuller cultivation of the spiritual qualities of man. Whatever we think about their origin, as scientists we should no longer sneer at or ignore them, for on their strength depends our own survival. There is something in them which is deeper than

intellect and rises from within, little subject to reason or to logic. Unless these inner forces can be tamed and cultivated till they will help us guide our course, we shall destroy ourselves.

Whatever was new in Sinnott's discourse came more from the occasion than from the sentiments. Jefferson himself had remarked in 1815, as the conflagration of the Napoleonic wars burned itself out: "I fear from the experience of the last twenty-five years that morals do not of necessity advance hand in hand with the sciences." From Jefferson, Sinnott had moved to Emerson. Sinnott introduced into his discourse that old nonscientific Emersonian word, intuition. Disregarding the skepticism of Krutch, Sinnott even suggested the intuition of the poet as an authentic source of wisdom. Though the director of the Sheffield Scientific School spoke at a time when Americans faced a novel and unprecedented crisis, his thought was strangely familiar. It seemed to reflect a current of ideas, flowing sometimes below the surface, that in America had come down from older decades. Intuition of what? From at least as long ago as the eighteenth century, Americans have held fast to the intuitive belief in the innate capacity of human nature to achieve sufficient wisdom and virtue to make an ordered and humane society possible. This assumption, moreover, though often not consciously recognized, underlay, by a curious paradox, even twentieth-century naturalism. It helps to account for the fact that during these decades naturalistic rationalism in America, whether expressed in the literary creation of a Clemens or a Dreiser or in social and political thinking, was almost always enlisted in the cause of human betterment. The Nazi leadership on the contrary, as demonstrated by Dachau and Buchenwald, carried the logic of Darwinian naturalism to its ultimate conclusion, extermination of a hated rival group.

Mr. Justice Holmes, prophet of legal realism, illustrates an unreconciled ambivalence in American thought in the interwar period. As a young man just out of the university in the 1860s, he had fought through four years of fratricidal strife and had thrice been wounded. Though Jerome Frank called him the greatest among the adult agnostics of his generation, Holmes founded his thought on a humanistic faith that grew out of intuition. "I do not know what is true," he remarked on one occasion. "I do not know the meaning of the universe. But in the midst of doubt, in the collapse of creeds, there is always one thing I do not doubt. . . . Most men who know battle know the cynic force with which the thoughts of common sense will assail them in times of stress; but they know that in their greatest moments faith has trampled those thoughts under foot . . . if you have known the vicissitudes of terror and of triumph in war, you know there is such a thing as the faith I spoke of. You know your own weakness and are modest; but you know that man has in him that unspeakable somewhat which makes him capable of miracle, able to lift himself by the might of his own soul, unaided, able to face annihilation for a blind belief." Holmes put his faith in freedom, the "free trade of ideas in the market."

Robert Frost, poet of the New England uplands, had also his own personal intuitive understanding of innate qualities of human nature. In the heyday of the prestige of the scientific outlook between the wars, he had quietly spoofed, in "The White-tailed Hornet," some of the assumptions that underlay that world view. He concluded with a comment on what so many of his contemporaries classified as realism.

Our worship, humor, conscientiousness
Went long since to the dogs under the table.
And served us right for having instituted
Downward comparisons. As long on earth
As our comparisons were stoutly upward
With gods and angels, we were men at least,

But little lower than the gods and angels.
But once comparisons were yielded downward,
Once we began to see our images
Reflected in the mud and even dust,
'Twas disillusion upon disillusion.
We were lost piecemeal to the animals,
Likę people thrown out to delay the wolves.
Nothing but fallibility was left us. . . .

Perhaps Sinnott had been reading Frost before he talked to his fellow scientists.

Holmes and Frost illustrate the current of humanistic thinking that has flowed in America without break from Jefferson's eighteenth century to the present. Both Holmes and Frost emphasized its basic tenet, namely that only ideals and values, tenaciously held, can control power. When the thunderheads of the antihumanistic philosophies and practices of totalitarianism blackened the twentieth-century skies, Americans in 1943 built beside the Potomac a new temple to an old faith. Six years later Vannevar Bush spelled out that faith in an age in which the reason of man had achieved the eighteenth-century goal and had penetrated to one of the ultimate secrets of the Author of Nature. "The outcome," he said, speaking of the Cold War, "will depend on faith, faith that there is more to a philosophy of life and more to the nature of man than harsh, selfish struggle for survival and dominion."

Bush spoke of qualities of universal human nature; he emphasized values that have validity beyond the limits of the jurisdiction. At the same time he gave informed advice to his fellow citizens on the development of national military power. The two aspects of Bush's thought emphasize the dichotomy in the thinking of the present age. When science lifted the lid of Pandora's atom, the logic of global cooperation became insistent. Atomic energy must be internationally controlled. But the logic of geopolitics did not disappear. If the conclusions of geopolitics are sound, moreover, fate is on the side of the power that controls the heart-land of the Eurasian continent and that power can afford to wait to establish its own pattern of global cooperation. As in the period between the wars, there is a strain toward consistency in the thought of our post-Hiroshima years, a strain toward universalism on a shrunken globe. The question is: what universalism, that which rests primarily on power extended to encompass the earth or that which bases itself ultimately on a faith in humane values applicable to all men everywhere?

At the dinner with the Polish representative that night in Washington in 1944, the conversation had run to subjugated Poland, victim of the politics of power. As I said goodbye to my host, I sensed that it was a wistful hope that caused him to take his friends to the Jefferson Memorial, a hope that the ideas expressed there in bronze and stone would one day prevail for his people and his country. Since that day the sky has become even darker than it then was. The long record in the history of the West, however, of the achievements of the free mind and the humane spirit suggests that fate is on the side of the exiled Pole. Human nature being what it is, man can yet, with patience and determination, use freedom and humane ideals to subdue power to civilization.

7

Nationalism and the Atom

World War II had ended. The press had published the pictures of Hiroshima. James Conant, president of Harvard, sat, on October 9, 1945, before a tense Committee on Military Affairs of the House of Representatives. "Perhaps you could realize the potential dangers to the Nation—," he said, "the potential good also for civilization—that may be involved in this tremendous energy, only if you had been, as I was, at the test of the bomb at Alamogordo Air Base on that morning in July, and seen the effect, that tremendous illumination that burst all over the sky, which so surprised even those who had been anticipating the explosion and knew all about it in advance. As Dr. Vannevar Bush has said, we are entering a new world."

Since that October after the war, more than a decade of scientific and technological advance has conditioned our thinking, together with our emotional and, perhaps, even our moral responses. We

SOURCE: Reprinted, with permission, from *The Virginia Quarterly Review* 33, No. 4 (Fall 1957): 539-548.

have become familiar with the pictures of the mushroom cloud. We have seen the first atom bomb so far surpassed that we have acquired an immunity to surprise. We have accepted the idea that, if necessary, we will bring down mass destruction of property and life upon our enemy. The "new world" tends to become commonplace. Yet the issues raised by the sudden appearance of nuclear power remain unaltered. It is useful to look at them as they appeared to the men who, without precedents to fall back on, prepared for the first time to make decisions concerning them.

"Science is not destructive as a whole," said Irving Langmuir of General Electric on November 30, 1945, as he faced a barrage of anxious and almost angry questions from the Special Committee on Atomic Energy of the United States Senate. "Our standards of living, our whole existence of America," Langmuir continued defensively, "has been developed by science. . . . We cannot have a holiday in science because we don't like certain aspects of science, because science only discovers the facts of nature." Langmuir's remark referred to a sudden and widespread popular revulsion against science that had produced a Frankenstein monster. "England is not going to have a holiday in science, if we do," the witness went on; "Russia isn't; France isn't; and if we stop progress and stagnate, we will deserve to be exterminated in fifty years. We should just clutter up the world uselessly." A member of the committee, Senator Edwin C. Johnson of Colorado, replied to Langmuir with equal earnestness. "Of course I believe that with all my heart," he said. "I believe our security lies in the laboratory and in scientific development, that is my religion. . . ." Johnson was one of a large company of Americans who, in spite of the fact that science had produced an instrument of death of almost infinite possibilities, still believed that scientific advance offered the one hope of survival. Significantly, both Langmuir and Johnson thought in the terms of a traditional nationalism.

Another witness, John A. Simpson, looked at the emerging issues of the atomic age differently. He spoke as chairman of the

Executive Committee of Atomic Scientists of Chicago. He described for the senators one of the most poignant moments in history. He told of the time only a few weeks back when laboratory men gathered in little groups for discussion as the success of the Manhattan Project became more and more probable. "As a result of these discussions," said Simpson, "there developed among many of the men of the laboratories a strong sense of responsibility—a responsibility which in many respects is unique in history, because, for the first time in history a new age lay in the hands of a relatively few men unknown to the rest of the world." Could these men of the project thrust upon the world the development they were bringing to a conclusion without assuming the obligation of informing the American people of changes they must face if they were to survive? They thought not. "As scientists," Simpson went on, "we have always preferred to have the results of our studies used for constructive rather than destructive purposes. . . [but] we have not heretofore felt our responsibility to strive for this rational use of the fruits of our labor." In matter-of-fact language that contrasted with the revolutionary character of the proposal, Simpson gave to the committee his own conclusions and those of his colleagues. "The United States," he said, "has a fleeting opportunity to insist on the only solution acceptable to a nation committed to peace. . . . Irrespective of other international agreements, we feel that international or world control of atomic energy is essential to the maintenance of peace. Such a system of effective controls implemented by inspection should be considered immediately." When the young scientist had finished, the chairman expressed to him the particular thanks of the committee. Simpson and his colleagues had declared in effect that the harnessing of nuclear energy had outmoded the freewheeling nationalism of the nineteenth century.

One of the great moments in the history of American foreign policy came several months later when Bernard Baruch, speaking as the representative of the one nation possessing atomic power, addressed the opening session of the Atomic Commission of the United Nations. "Behind the black portent of the atomic age," said Baruch, "lies a hope which, seized upon with faith, can work salvation. If we fail, then we have damned every man to be the slave of fear. . . . The United States proposes an international atomic development authority, to which should be entrusted all phases of the development and use of atomic energy."

Joseph Stalin directed the Soviet representative to oppose the American plan. Thanks, in part, to the information supplied secretly by Klaus Fuchs, Russia had already made progress toward the production of an atomic bomb. The new weapon had put the United States in the number one power position in the world. The Communist dictator refused to accept second place. He rejected an international plan that would have limited his freedom of action with respect to nuclear energy. He chose the path of nationalism. As a result, possession of the bomb and of the power that went with it became overnight the measure of national prestige. The history of the "new world" of which Vannevar Bush spoke began with a paradox. The harnessing of nuclear energy had at the same time intensified nationalism and made its traditional nineteenth-century version an anachronism.

II

Although many elements enter into the sentiment of nationalism and though these vary from people to people, one is basic and universal. Louis L. Snyder at the end of his illuminating study has described it. "It [nationalism] is," he says, "that socially approved symbol used by modern society in its search for security."

The appearance of the absolute weapon had varied implications for security. During the brief period in which the United States had a monopoly of atomic power, the American people enjoyed an invincible security. Partly out of generosity to nations wounded by war and partly in the furtherance of the national interest, they extended their atomic shield to include Western Europe. When the Soviet Union developed the bomb, the problem of security underwent a radical transformation. It became impossible for either the U.S.S.R. or the U.S.A. in the event of a nuclear war to preserve its cities or its people from destruction. In the nuclear age the nation-state could no longer perform its primary task in a shooting war. The logic of the situation called for collective security global in character. But the chasm that divided the free world from the Communist empire could not be bridged. The Baruch proposal having failed, the United States fell back on the nationalistic solution of building up armament, capable of immediate and lethal action, as a deterrent to possible aggression. The atomic stalemate came into being and with it what Winston Churchill called the "balance of terror."

The situation intensified nationalism. The bombs, at first atomic and then hydrogen, had no value unless they could be delivered over a chosen target. A race in the development and production of aircraft and guided missiles came into being. Under the new conditions security for the nation depended upon preventing the adversary from gaining a commanding lead in either or both of these carriers of atomic warheads. The old-style armament race with all its evils and dangers reappeared in the middle of the twentieth century. A swollen budget and the burden of high taxes stood high among the evils. But the armament race of the 1950s differed from earlier competitions in one important particular. There was an element of absurdity in pouring wealth into the creation of better missiles and better aircraft for use in a possible war which no nation could win and in which all participants must lose. But, absurd or not, the conditions of the world required the development of deterrent armament to the full extent that evolving science and technology made possible.

In 1957 the United Kingdom detonated a hydrogen bomb over Christmas Island. A nation whose empire had been disintegrating and whose influence had declined in areas vital to her economy regained in the moment of that explosion her place among the major world powers. The event gave to the British people a badly needed psychological lift. The episode suggests a relation in our time between nationalism and the atom. The menace of the bomb has not been able to compel the nations to surrender control of the weapon through some form of international arrangement. On the contrary, the existence of the bomb has caused at least some of the have-not nations to covet it. French scientists are working to make their nation a nuclear power. Less than a decade and a half has passed since the explosion at Alamogordo. What may happen even in the first half century of the atomic era in the spread of nuclear armament in the society of nations is beyond the possibility of useful speculation. The answer depends on whether or not international controls can be established.

III

In 1956 and 1957 the extensive testing of nuclear weapons by Russia, the United States, and Britain made the present generation suddenly conscious of the one world of the upper atmosphere. The fallout and, in particular, the malevolent strontium 90, drifting here and there, fell alike on friend, neutral, and foe—not to mention ourselves. The outcry that came from many nations and in particular from the British and American peoples embarrassed at least the governments of those two nations. Pressures built up to stop the testing and so reduce the threat of bone cancer and of an increase in genetic malformations in future generations. The perils peculiar to a race in nuclear armament became a potent influence for undertaking a first step in international control. In the event of failure, the governments of the Western democracies had to appeal to their peoples to accept the new peril from the heavens as the price of national security. The Communist police state did not need to make such an appeal; the Soviet government did not even inform its people that it was making nuclear tests. In effect, the officials in Western governments charged with responsibility for defense asked the citizens to accept known hazards in the hope that the improvement of nuclear weapons would prevent the war which, if it came, all nations must lose. Tenuous as it was, the appeal had validity. Moreover, it offered the only possibility if security policies were to be developed along wholly nationalistic lines. A defect of the policy lay in what might be called the area of public relations of the nuclear powers. The peoples of the nations that did not possess bombs inevitably looked with a jaundiced eye on the necessity of accepting the perils of hot rain in order that another country might be more secure. The reality of the one world of the upper atmosphere and the free flow of the fallout within it exerted a most powerful pressure, particularly on Britain and the United States, who, rather than attempt to conceal, frankly announced their tests.

The uproar over the dangers of testing brought out manifestations of nationalism similar to that of the time of fear when the McCarthy investigations took place. The press reported a comment of an unnamed high American official. "In all this agitation against nuclear tests," the officer remarked, "there has been a series of curious coincidences. Certain people seem to be very quiet whenever Russia tests a nuclear weapon, but seem very vocal when the U. S. makes a test." A similar comment came from Britain, once so critical of what they thought to be an American inclination to look for a Communist under every bed. "The leaders of this campaign [against British nuclear tests]," said the late Viscount Cherwell, scientist and member of the British Atomic Energy Authority, "are certainly a very curious collection. Oddly enough, none of them seems to worry very much about the Russian tests. . . . It is the British tests they insist will poison the world." Undoubtedly there was some truth in the implied accusations. It is a matter of public record that, after completing their unannounced series of tests, the Russians, with customary cynicism, began beating the propaganda drums and demanding in the name of humanity the end of testing. But a nationalism that tended to dismiss all criticism of testing as Communist-inspired was a nationalism showing its evil side. An event unexpected by the public prevented this particular evil from becoming important.

The scene changed when key American scientists briefed the President and informed him that the Atomic Energy Commission had nearly achieved a virtually clean bomb. The public pressure to end testing declined. Russian efforts to discredit the announcement suggested its importance. The armament race could continue with a minimum of embarrassment for the United Kingdom and the United States. In fact, the effort to produce the clean bomb, which began as far back as 1954, seems to have been part of the armament race. When ground forces use atomic artillery and other atomic weapons to facilitate advance, the military importance of clean bombs is obvious. One suspects that the clamor over the fallout compelled the disclosure of a military secret. Suffice it to say that, if we must have primarily nationalistic solutions for the problem of national security, the news of the clean bomb furthered such solutions.

IV

The long-continued failure of the London disarmament negotiations to achieve a first step in halting the building and accumulation of nuclear weapons for a war that both antagonists consider would be suicidal suggests the persistence and strength of nationalism in an atomic age. The Western powers, to be sure, recognizing the cost and dangers of the armament race, have announced their willingness to accept such limits on their sovereignty as would be imposed by international inspectors charged with guaranteeing a treaty. The offer may be accepted as genuine. The Soviet Union has made a similar proposal—in words. But for more than a decade, the Russians have refused to enter into any arrangement that would not in some vital particular give the U.S.S.R. freedom of action. This principle of freedom of action inhered in the long-standing Russian proposal that both sides pledge to one another that they would not use nuclear weapons. The rulers of the Soviet Union must, of necessity, view such a pledge in the context of the first precept of Communist ethics, namely, that that which advances the revolution is the supreme good. The Soviet theory that Russia is the originator and center of world communism makes the precept applicable to Russian nationalism. In the light of this overriding rule of action, a solemn commitment need be no limitation on freedom of action and, in fact, might well become a stratagem for Communist and national aggression.

The Cold War between the West and its Communist adversary continues in a world in which nationalisms, old and new, undergo development and change. A new nationalism burgeons in the Gold Coast. In Europe some of the most ancient nations accept limitations on freedom of action as they move toward economic union and the acceptance of Euratron. The United Nations on occasion has been the instrument for imposing limits on the activities of small and even of great nations. But one must look at the reality that lay behind what appeared to be a great triumph for the United Nations in 1956. When that organization forced the withdrawal of Israel, France, and Great Britain from Egyptian territory, the visible possibility of a brushfire blazing into a general nuclear war provided the ultimate sanction. It is the same sanction that makes the balance of terror an instrument of peace. But the policymakers of the United States, recognizing that such security as is possible for our nation in this atomic age must be achieved through collective undertakings, develop American policy within the framework of the United Nations. By so doing our government has accepted the principle that security must be sought through collective effort involving some genuine surrender of power.

Our nation cannot carry on successfully in its efforts to protect our citizens without allies. NATO provides essential defense for the United States as well as that of other member nations. As they face the Communist menace, the fate of all is involved in the fate of one. The conditions of the contemporary world, in which a hostile nation can strike a devastating blow in a matter of hours, impose limitations upon the freedom of action even of the United States, one of the two superpowers of the atomic age. As a consequence, American nationalism expresses itself within the limits set by the needs of collective security. The decision of the Supreme Court in the Girard case[1] established some of those limits in law. The understandable demand of large numbers of our citizens that Girard be tried by Americans in accordance with American usage did not prevail against the hard necessities created by the international situation. But, if the expression of American nationalism is cribbed and confined, its essential character and importance remain unimpaired. Though such things cannot be measured, it seems accurate to say that the intensity of our nationalism in the 1950s, a time of great danger, surpasses that of the 1850s, when threats from abroad were unimportant. In the atomic age Americans still look primarily to their own nation for security.

The scientists of the Manhattan Project in 1945 thought that the atom bomb they were putting together would make the old nationalism an anachronism. What they did not foresee was that an atomic stalemate would permit hostile nations to survive from day to day. Perhaps they will survive long enough to permit the Russians to rid themselves of the Communist aberration. Human nature being what it is, one has difficulty not to believe that one day this great people will achieve freedom. Even if liberation does not occur, perhaps one day the hard logic of the atomic age will force all nations into genuine and effective measures for collective security. If and when that event occurs, it seems clear that nationalism, though limited and confined, will motivate the policies of the powers. What seems already to be emerging is a blend of nationalism and internationalism. The force released from the atom has not made and will not in the foreseeable future make nationalism a complete anachronism. What the release of atomic energy has compelled is the development in international society of arrangements that, avoiding the extremes of freewheeling nationalism and world government, establish a compromise between the two.

Notes

[1] Wilson, Secretary of Defense et al. *v.* Girard. July 11, 1957, *United States Reports* Vol. 354, October term, 1956. Girard, a member of the American armed forces stationed in Japan, while on duty guarding a machine gun on a firing range, fired from a grenade launcher an empty cartridge case which struck and killed a Japanese woman whom he suspected of gathering empty shells. Under the Security Treaty between the United States and Japan, an administrative agreement had been drawn up which recognized concurrent jurisdiction on the part of the two nations. Under this agreement, local American authorities declared that because Girard had acted in performance of official duty he should be tried in an American court. Japanese authorities contended that he had acted beyond the scope of official duty and, therefore, Japan had the "primary right" to exercise jurisdiction. The affair was widely publicized by the news media in the United States and attracted great public interest at a time when the memories of a long, bitter, and bloody war were still fresh.

After negotiation, the United States authorities, with the approval of the President, waved jurisdiction and prepared to deliver Girard to Japanese authorities. The Japanese court indicted Girard for murder. Girard's attorneys sought relief in the United States District Court in the District of Columbia. That court refused to grant a writ of *habeas corpus* but issued an injunction against Girard's delivery to Japanese authorities. The Supreme Court upheld the refusal of the lower court to grant a writ of *habeas corpus* but reversed the injunction. It affirmed that the wisdom of arrangements made under the authority of the Security Treaty which granted qualified jurisdiction to Japan in the matter of American armed forces was "exclusively for the determination of the Executive and Legislative Branches."

8

The Cold War and Changes in American Thought

In June 1958, university classes that graduated in 1913 found themselves forty-five years out of college. They were the last of the classes to graduate at a time when the thought patterns of the nineteenth century were still dominant. These university men were, in fact, members of a dwindling company who linked an old America to a new nation.

The year 1913 came at the climax of what historians call the Progressive Era. Woodrow Wilson had been inaugurated in March preceding their commencement in June. It was a time of looking forward, of belief in the glorious possibilities of the future. Progress was one of the key words of the time. And progress meant to leave the old and outmoded behind and to press on to something

SOURCE: Reprinted, with permission, from *The Virginia Quarterly Review* 35, No. 1 (Winter 1959): 53-63.

new. Both Theodore Roosevelt and Woodrow Wilson defined Progressivism in terms of moral as well as material and political advance. Early in the century, grave social and political evils had been disclosed—particularly in the cities. Some cleanup campaigns had succeeded and corruption had been punished. Perhaps the most spectacular was the crusade of young Charles Evans Hughes against evil doing in the insurance companies. The churches, particularly those in the rapidly growing cities, emphasized the social gospel.

The developments of the time seemed to confirm and strengthen the doctrines of the American democratic faith that had taken form in the first half of the nineteenth century. That faith emphasized three doctrines in particular: the doctrine of the fundamental law, of the free and responsible individual, and of the mission of America. The concept of the fundamental law was partly political and partly moral. It stemmed from the doctrine of natural rights —the right to life, liberty, and the pursuit of happiness that Jefferson wrote into the Declaration of Independence. These rights were part of a fundamental law of nature underlying society. This idea of a natural law originated in ancient Greece. The American doctrine of the fundamental law stemmed also from the doctrine of the moral law of God that is basic to our Judeo-Christian tradition. In either case it was thought of as a law not made by men, but rather as a law that contained the principles of humane living and the precepts for the government of a humane society. The second doctrine of the democratic faith was that of the free and responsible individual: the individual free to work out his personal destiny and free to make of his life what his abilities and opportunities made possible, and responsible ultimately to the fundamental law which insisted that the liberty of the individual did not extend to the willful impairment of that of his fellows. Ralph Waldo Emerson in the first half of the nineteenth century had been the chief prophet of both doctrines—that of the existence of a moral order fundamental to the cosmos and of the vast capacities of the free individual within that order if he would but realize the powers existing within his own heart. Emerson had seen the free political institutions of America as the expression in government of the democratic faith. He recognized that this expression was imperfect in practice but he insisted that the chief goal of free political institutions was to further the emergence and development of self-reliant individuals. The third doctrine of the old democratic faith had to do with the nation. It insisted that the American people, organized as a nation, had a mission to stand before the world as a witness that free men can govern themselves without the aid of kings or of an hereditary aristocracy.

The men of the nineteenth century, down to and including the classes which graduated in 1913, assumed that the future lay with democracy, that it would one day triumph in the world. In the nineteenth century, Western Europe was the power center of the world. Liberal political institutions were old in England. After the American and the French Revolutions at the end of the eighteenth century, liberal parliamentary government made great progress on the European continent. To Americans the growth of liberal institutions in Europe seemed to presage the ultimate triumph of democratic institutions in the less advanced portions of the world. Down to 1913 the United States was still a relatively remote nation, remote from the great powers of Europe and from the teeming populations of Japan, China, and India. Two broad oceans gave us security against any serious threat from overseas. And in the Western Hemisphere no potential enemy menaced our peace. In isolation and with a sense of security we made domestic affairs our primary interest, avoided international entanglements, and developed our democratic institutions in the confident hope of the ultimate world triumph of those liberal and humane principles which we espoused and which had made such progress in Europe.

When the classes of 1918 left college, World War I was almost four years old and, with America participating, had reached its final climactic year. Most of the men of these classes, of course, did not leave college in 1918—but earlier, to join what the President of the United States called a crusade to save democracy in Europe against an autocratic militarism and, by extending the democratic principle to the field of international organization, to put an end to the use of violence among the great nations as a means of settling their disputes.

But after 1919 the hopes of Wilsonian idealism faded. And a bitter disillusionment with Europe bred a conscious and magnified isolationism. As the years ran on, it became increasingly clear that World War I had opened a new epoch—but not of peace ensured by democracy. Rather, World War I initiated an age of revolutions and of wars on a scale unprecedented in history. Not the least of the transformations had to do with the position of the United States in the society of nations. Twenty-eight years after our entry into World War I, the United States emerged from World War II victorious in a global conflict and, by virtue of a momentary monopoly of the atom bomb, the most powerful nation in the world. Our country was, in fact, possessed of such power as no nation previously had ever had. The immediate background of the changes with which this essay is concerned may be found in these twenty-eight years of violence, depression, and again violence. But it seems useful to concentrate on the years after World War II, in particular the 1950s, when a cold war between the United States and the U.S.S.R. made clear the realities of national existence in the nuclear age.

How has this cold war forced modification, or reorientation, or change of emphasis in American thinking? It is a crucial question. Some suggestions only are offered here.

Let us begin by looking at our nation as a member of the society of nations. For the first time in our history, we face in a time of theoretical peace an enemy who is determined, implacable, willing to wait to achieve his ends, and possessed of power at least equal to our own. I am reminded of more than a century of European history when Germany and France faced one another across an anxious border. France and Germany seemed giants to the members of the classes of 1913 when they were in college. Less than half a century later their old and unremitting contention is dwarfed by that between the mid-twentieth-century colossi, the United States and the U.S.S.R. As a result of this contention has come a revolution in American thinking that has to do with the expectancy of war itself. In the course of our national history we have fought many wars—the War of 1812, the Mexican War, the Civil War, the Spanish-American War. Each one of these was unexpected. And we came to the brink of each quite unprepared. In 1861, when the nation divided, the regular army of the United States numbered 13,000 men, scattered on police duty throughout a vast expanse of Indian country in the West. In the nineteenth century, when we felt secure, peace was the normal expectation for Americans. Wars were ugly emergencies to be dealt with by armies of volunteers answering the call to national service. But now the situation is reversed. A state of cold war has become normal. Most of us are convinced that only what Winston Churchill called a balance of terror protects us from the actual bombs. But war has become total war. The campaigns of the Cold War are waged in the fields of diplomacy, of economics, of propaganda. And no one can see the end. One recalls the song of the Civil War that was sung by both Federals and Confederates—"Tenting on the Old Camp Ground." We remember the refrain: "Waiting for the war to cease, Waiting for the dawn of peace." That hope has been the normal attitude of Americans in every war save, I believe, the present Cold War. Today we hope that it may be possible to ease the tension a little. But we have no reasonable grounds for expecting that in the foreseeable future the American people will enjoy the modicum of peace and the sense of security that we enjoyed before August 1914. I see nothing to be gained by bemoaning the change. A look at the long span of history, particularly of Europe, suggests the idea that tension and conflict are more nearly normal conditions than that century of security Americans enjoyed from 1815 to 1914. Events force us to learn to live with danger, insecurity, and anxiety. Our free institutions were matured in the century of security. Their present and future evolution must be against a background of insecurity. The realization of this fact seems to me to be the greatest and most revolutionary change in American thought brought about by the conditions of the mid-twentieth century.

I would suggest briefly what seem to me to be some of the byproducts of this change: the abandonment of isolationism as a policy of security; the cultivation of allies and the forging of alliances, such as NATO and SEATO; the evolution of the old idea of the mission of America. Events both within and without the United States have brought our nation into a position of leadership in the free world. Our national mission is no longer merely to stand in our isolated continent as witness to the efficacy and desirability of free and democratic institutions but to play the commanding rôle in a continuing conflict for their preservation. The conditions of the mid-twentieth century have transformed the mission of America into that of leadership in a fight for survival of the free world.

There is another byproduct that inheres in the phrase "massive retaliation." Our defense and that of our ally Britain assumes our willingness as a people, in a possible time of extremity, to loose upon an enemy people the mass destruction of property and human life involved in the detonation of the hydrogen bomb. The conditions of our world give us no alternative. We have cause to believe that our enemy is ruthless. I do not pretend to be able to answer the question of what is the significance for the old doctrine of the fundamental law of this willingness to use the ultimate weapon. It is a matter of record that, in spite of the cogent reasons advanced by Mr. Stimson and Mr. Truman for Hiroshima, our national conscience is still uneasy at our having pioneered in the dropping of the atom bomb. Our adjustment to this moral problem involved in the possible use of the hydrogen bomb seems to be to emphasize that the requirements of survival force our hand, to trust that the balance of nuclear terror will prevent the major nuclear war, and to bend our energies to the task of slowing down or ending the race in missiles. Concentrating on these beliefs and activities, we put out of our minds the possibility of the ultimate possible decision. But we would do well to remember that a moral dilemma lies at the heart of our present civilization. Our forefathers thought of progress, among other things, as increasing apprehension of the requirements of the fundamental moral law and the consequent development of human sympathy and humanitarian activities. In the nineteenth century and in the Progressive Era at the beginning of the twentieth, the idea of progress produced an easy and shallow optimism, and sometimes even utopian hopes. It is hard to say what is happening to the idea of progress in the present day. Today Reinhold Niebuhr is only one among many who insist on the toughness and persistence of evil in human life. As we move forward in the third quarter of the twentieth century, we have a new understanding of the magnitude of the problem of evil we have to deal with. Social and ethical thought in America is acquiring, in my opinion, a depth and sophistication far beyond that of the nineteenth century. We are, as we were in the nineteenth century, a generous and humanitarian people. The United Funds or Community Chests in our cities large and small have no real counterpart anywhere else in the world. The development of our social sciences has made our work of relief and rehabilitation vastly more intelligent than that of the agencies supported by the alms of seventy-five years ago. Yet we of the latter half of the twentieth century have long since given up that illusion of the eighteenth-century Enlightenment that human nature can be perfected. We hold fast, however, to our ideals of a humane civilization. And, in spite of the occasional frightening manifestation of barbarism in our midst, we do a fair job in maintaining a decent society in which men and women can live constructive and useful lives. Yet we are quite prepared to loose, if we have to, the frightfulness of the ultimate weapon upon our adversary. The Cold War has caused us to live in the midst of a paradox from which we can see no escape. One wonders what the effect of this paradox on our people will be if it continues half a century.

The strains of the Cold War have brought into the open many of the fundamental facts of life. I will mention a few. All are recognized by those among us who take time to think. The management of a highly complex industrial society requires a strong government. To counter effectively the aggressions and maneuvers of our powerful totalitarian enemy requires not only a strong government but one capable of acting with split-second timing. The concentration of vast power in government tends to dwarf the individual. If we permit the individual to be swallowed up by the state, we take on the character of our enemy and by so doing surrender to him. We deal, moreover, with a nation and a system that have developed the technique of subversion and infiltration beyond the achievements of any other power in history. The stakes in this international competition between the Soviet Union and ourselves are beyond calculation. For this reason alone we know that our adversary seeks constantly to infiltrate our defenses. Yet we hold with Emerson that the ultimate strength of the nation lies in the strength of the individual men and women who comprise it. We cannot meet the threat of infiltration and subversion by the methods of the police state. Our experiences in the 1950s have taught us that we must set the authority of the individual beside the authority of the state. And the authority of the individual springs from his freedom, his trained intelligence, and his character. At the time of the Korean War and of the Hiss and Coplon trials many of us were panicked into an effort to defend our government and our civilization against the subversive and the infiltrator by flouting the basic freedoms and denying the basic rights of the individual. The ordeal of McCarthyism in the early 1950s was our lesson in the complexities of the attempt to strike a balance between the goal of security for the nation and security for those rights of the individual which give dignity to human life. One consequence of the Cold War against imperial communism has been to give this mid-twentieth-century generation an understanding of the realities and the difficulties of democracy surpassing that of any of its predecessors.

There are two more areas in which the exigencies of the Cold War have brought us a sharpened perception of the problems associated with our democratic way of life. The first is education. Our traditional ideal of the free and responsible individual citizen and the fundamental principle of our nation, namely, government by the consent of the governed, have worked together from the beginning of our history as a nation to further the cause of education among us. In contrast to the traditional practice of nineteenth-century Europe, we adopted the principle of education for all the people in the nineteenth century. In that century we developed mass education at the level of the primary school. In the first half of the twentieth century, we extended mass education to the secondary school. In the second half of the twentieth century, something like mass education seems to be extending to the university level. The controlling ideal has been to give each child as he starts his life career as nearly as possible equality of opportunity. We have assumed properly that government by consent of the governed cannot work unless the governed are sufficiently informed to arrive at reasonable and sound decisions.

But mass education has its limitations; in fact, it poses grave problems for the survival of the democratic system. The inevitable tendency of democratically controlled mass education is to train the mediocre and to let the brilliant child more or less shift for himself after he has accomplished the tasks set for his less gifted classmates. Too often he never achieves his full potentialities. But as the technology of our civilization has become vastly complicated and as the problems of government and society have also become vastly complicated, we have become increasingly aware of the importance for the nation of the above-average citizen—the citizen above average in intellectual ability and in training. Our thought as a people has been dominated by the cult of the average, and the glorification of the average. We have given the semicontemptuous names, highbrow and egghead, to the exceptional. In 1957 the appearance of Sputnik I in the heavens and the consequent near calamitous decline of American prestige throughout the world brought us face to face with some of the facts of life in the second half of the twentieth century. These are that if our democratic system is to be saved, it must be by men and women of superior intelligence and training. Clearly, we must hold fast to the principle of educating the masses of the citizens. But we are compelled to superimpose on mass education the special training required by the gifted. The task is staggering. In spite of the volume of discussion that has followed Sputnik I, there is as yet no conclusive evidence that the masses of our people are sufficiently awake to the needs of the hour to make the necessary changes in their attitude toward eggheads or the necessary sacrifices to adapt our educational system to the requirements of an infinitely dangerous hour. Unless they do, we cannot take the survival of our free institutions for granted—perhaps not even then.

Another area in which the exigencies of the Cold War have brought sharpened perceptions is in that of race relations. Our enemy has exploited to our great disadvantage our failures in this regard. The greatest glory of American democracy in the present time is to be found in the fact that a majority of our people have come squarely to grips with the most difficult of all social problems, the relation between the white and the Negro races. Particularly since World War II in this area the Declaration of Independence has functioned as a national conscience. We have sought to give reality to the asserted inherent rights of life, liberty, and the pursuit of happiness. Events have made clear the almost insurmountable difficulties of the problem. But the events have not shaken the determination of a majority of our people to give reality for all our people to that central principle of democracy, namely the dignity of the individual person. In this we are far advanced beyond the positions our people had achieved in 1913. As I read the thought of our present time, we have in our announced purposes and our practical actions treated the principle of the dignity of man as part of the fundamental law that we assume to have validity in all times and places.

Wars set up strains that test the strength and disclose the weaknesses of a civilization. The Cold War in which we are engaged is no exception. It provides an even harder test because it is devoid of heroics. It can be argued that, on balance, it has been an advantage to us. It has required us to think deeply on the full meaning of freedom for the individual and on the most desirable relation of the individual to the state. The Cold War has taught us beyond the possibility of misunderstanding our dependence not only upon the trained intelligence and the probity of the masses but upon the work of the abler and specially trained few. The denial of humane principles on the part of our enemy—one thinks of Hungary—has intensified our devotion to the ideal of achieving and maintaining a humane society. At the same time hard realities of the present age have given us a sophistication born of the understanding of the difficulties in the way of achieving the good society. This understanding, by putting an end to naiveté, is, I believe, an advantage. Whether we have the will as a people to profit by the lesson remains for the future to disclose.

As a nation we have never yet lost a war. I do not believe that we will lose the present Cold War. We are supported by the knowledge that we defend noble principles that further life and make for a greater richness in living. In this contention against totalitarian communism, our side is right. And I am convinced that in the end right will prevail.

9

Change and New Perspectives

Americans have been on the move since migrants from Europe came ashore in the seventeenth century from the *Susan Constant* and the *Mayflower*. The newcomers built simple habitations between the shore and the forest. In the eighteenth century clusters of houses beside the beach evolved into thriving seaports and inland farmers pushed the outer edge of their fields westward to the Appalachians and northward to the White Mountains. Toward the end of that century the farmers and the townsmen of the seaports threw off colonial subordination and embarked upon the hazardous adventure of independence. In the nineteenth century the sons and grandsons of the signers of the Declaration of Independence, turning their backs on the Atlantic, moved on foot, on horseback,

SOURCE: Reprinted, with permission, from *American Studies in Transition*, ed. Marshall W. Fishwick (Philadelphia: University of Pennsylvania Press, 1964), p. 101-113. Copyright 1964 by the Trustees of the University of Pennsylvania. (Published in paperback by Houghton-Mifflin Company, 1969.)

by river boat and by covered wagon westward to the Pacific. They founded homes and established enterprises in an area as large as Europe. The historian of the American people, looking back over three centuries and a half, observes, first and last, change—a people on the march behind moving boundaries; a society passing from a limited to a complex ethnic composition and from enslaving a race toward the reality for that race of equality of opportunity; an economy evolving from a simple agrarianism to an advanced industrialism; a nation, beginning as a weak confederation of states on a continent remote from centers of Western civilization, achieving strength and finally surging into world leadership to become the protector of that civilization threatened by a ruthless power and by a materialistic philosophy and system. From the beginning of their history, accelerating change has been the massive fact in the culture of the American people. In this phenomenon lies America's uniqueness.

Change approaches a climax in the middle decades of the twentieth century. To gain a clearer understanding of the conditions of life for the present generation of Americans, it is useful to inquire into the factors which have been important in bringing about change in the past and are still significant. Three emerge: the accelerating increase in the body of knowledge, especially scientific and technological knowledge, which undergirds our civilization; the ever shifting cultural configurations and power manifestations in the world outside our borders, a societal environment to which we make adjustments; and a cluster of values within our civilization which have been so long and so tenaciously held as to amount to a national faith. These three, operating in the middle of the twentieth century, provide the essential perspectives for the present generation.

The *Susan Constant* and the *Mayflower* crossed the Atlantic in the century which saw in Europe, and particularly in England, that breakthrough in knowledge and thought which has been called the scientific revolution. From the beginning, American annals paced forward synchronously with those of modern science. But until the twentieth century was well advanced the great centers of scientific learning remained in Europe. With the exception of the solitary Josiah Willard Gibbs and one or two others, science in the United States remained primarily derivative. At the same time, however, in days when technology was relatively simple the ingenuity of American tinkerers brought about extraordinary advances in the artifacts of their civilization. As the twentieth century opened, the historian Henry Adams sensed the emergence of new scientific understandings. He pointed out to his countrymen the phenomenon of acceleration in man's acquisition of scientific knowledge. He noted the marriage of science and technology and the dynamism born of that union speeding up innovation continuously, remorselessly. In a disturbing metaphor Adams tried to drive home his conclusion, namely, that advance in knowledge and evolution in technology bring and must continue to bring profound changes in society. He saw, even in his own day, modern man grasping a live wire which made him dance to its pulsations but which he cannot let go. Events confirmed the accuracy of Henry Adams' insights.

Then the United States took its place beside Europe as a center for scientific advance. Laboratories in universities, in industry, and in governmental agencies turned out an ever increasing volume of research findings. The simple technology of the nineteenth century was left behind as new materials and new machines transformed the life of society, harnessed the energy of the atom, and made possible the systematic exploration of inner and outer space. The government of the United States made science the cornerstone of national defense. In a world which survived because a nuclear stalemate had been achieved, the United States government pushed research and development, the union of science and technology, to innovation and more innovation. In this context the perspective of Henry Adams becomes further clarified. We see the mid-twentieth-century American at the same time bending his efforts to push forward innovation and, summoning what wisdom he can, to adjust his life and society to swift, continuous, and compelling change. Within this larger picture two details stand out. One has to do with the fact that natural science has brought into being a body of knowledge staggering in extent, and the accumulation accelerates. The social sciences have added to the total. Inevitably the specialists emerged. The preoccupation of the specialist with the problems and tasks of his particular area of interest tended to generate in him parochialism both in loyalties and in outlook. Parochialism expressed itself in walls between intellectual disciplines. C. P. Snow in England discovered what he considered a deeper and more fundamental dichotomy. He pointed to a polarization between the sciences and the humanities which took the form of two cultures.

But the conditions of the modern world increasingly demand the wisdom and leadership of men who can transcend the limitations of a specialty or even of what Snow calls a culture. Perhaps because history as a discipline has a foot in both the social sciences and the humanities it was a historian who brought to the attention of teachers the importance of bringing the sciences and the humanities closer together. It had been achieved in the eighteenth century. The eighteenth-century man, such as Benjamin Franklin or Thomas Jefferson, had been a generalist in a simpler civilization and in an age when the body of scientific knowledge was small. His twentieth-century successor is, at the same time, more difficult to create and more needed by the times. The historian Joseph R. Strayer, aware of the importance of science and of the specialist for mid-twentieth-century life, has pointed out to members of his guild obligations they have to students and to the general public. "The post-Civil War period," Strayer remarked, "also gives an opportunity to take up a topic that is somewhat neglected even in our college courses—the emergence and growing importance of the scientific point of view. This should be more than a listing of scientific discoveries and theories, more even than a discussion of the impact of science on our way of life. What should be done, difficult though it may be, is to give some feeling for the scientist's way of looking at the world; some idea of the scientist's presuppositions and expectations. Thus, perhaps a start could be made in bridging the gap between scientific and humanistic cultures about which C. P. Snow has written so eloquently.'' (*The Social Studies and the Social Sciences*, sponsored by the American Council of Learned Societies and the National Council of Social Studies [New York: Harcourt Brace and World, 1962], p. 32.)

C. P. Snow dramatized a fault zone in modern Western civilization at a time when other men were becoming increasingly aware that such a separation of the humanities from the sciences is not only unnecessary but poses dangers to society. Strayer's charge to the teachers suggested an emerging new perspective. Human knowledge, in spite of all the boundaries which Balkanize it, is an interrelated whole. "Something there is which doesn't love a wall," wrote Robert Frost many years ago and then proceeded in poem after poem to translate the insights and understandings which he had received from science into lyrics. More recently a chemist, Harold G. Cassidy, remarked: "It is my thesis that the sciences and the arts, though different in many ways, are not mutually exclusive or fundamentally contradictory. They are complementary parts of our culture; loss or injury to one is a damage to others and the whole; neither the scientist nor the humanist need fear to respect the other. In fact in their mutual understanding lie the possibilities of unimagined cultural advances.'' (Harold Gomes Cassidy, *The Sciences and the Arts, a New Alliance* [New York: Harper and Brothers, 1962], p. 2.) Cassidy, Frost, and Strayer speak each from the background of his own specialty, science, the humanities, and history which combines both. In a civilization where change is far-reaching and swift they warn against schism. If the modern American is to live by reason, he must fuse the understandings and outlooks of science and the humanities. Dichotomy and mutual suspicion between them represents the failure of reason.

Mid-twentieth-century developments require the modern American to consider one especially among the "scientist's presuppositions and expectations." Within the corpus of the natural and the social sciences, cybernetics has emerged. The name may be freely translated as steersmanship. The steersman must have at command reliable information about the constantly changing effect of control measures. Feedback provides such information. "The brain, the sense, and the nervous system constitute a physiological cybernetic device. Fire directors, autopilots, computers, telephone networks, regulators, and a host of other engineering devices constitute examples of inorganic cybernetic instruments. There are basic laws of these devices which do not depend upon whether the apparatus is made of metal or protein molecules, and cyberneticians seek these laws." (Marshall Walker, *The Nature of Scientific Thought* [Englewood Cliffs, N. J.: Prentice-Hall, Inc., 1963], p. 95.) Cybernetics has made possible the machine to control machines. Only when the inanimate steersman fails, as it did for Gordon Cooper on the eve of his re-entry into the atmosphere, does man take over. Whereas formerly machines displaced the muscles of men and animals, now the robot governor displaces the mind of man. The "thinking machine," already powering changes of the greatest moment in American society, represents a dazzling triumph for its human creator. But the present generation asks: "What price automation?" Automation, displacing men at practically all levels of skill, has become a challenge to the human spirit. To cope with it and to keep it a beneficent force requires all the wisdom and the compassion which can be garnered from the sciences and the humanities together.

But cybernetics may be moving into other activities. The behavioral sciences, following the practice of the natural sciences, have begun to develop models in social science. Mathematics has been applied to economics and games theory to strategy in military operations. The psychologist, B. F. Skinner, believes that enough knowledge about the means of manipulating and controlling human behavior exists to make possible a last utopia, a Walden II, where science brings peace and happiness. Cybernetics provides a perspective for the mid-twentieth-century American from which to view and to take account of the changes in the world about him.

Automation, whether it be actual as in the machine, or suggested as for society, throws into relief the gap which C. P. Snow described between science and the humanities. The lore of the humanist includes the deposit left by the succession of vanished generations—art, literature, philosophical inquiries, ethical searching, worship. The vision of the humanist focuses on the individual person as a unique center of value, possessed of dignity when freed from external control, aspiring to ever further ranges in the development and expression of his powers. The lore and vision of the humanist exist in mid-twentieth-century American civilization beside the knowledge and understandings and techniques of the scientist. The two are parts of a single whole. In the words of Cassidy, "in their mutual understanding lie the possibilities of unimagined cultural advance."

Science brings about another quite different change which affects all the civilizations of the world. Since the time when *homo sapiens* became also *homo faber*, mankind has created a profusion of differing cultures. The variety among these cultures attests to the creative capacity of the human spirit. In such a world, modern science, originating in the West, spreads over the globe from laboratory to laboratory and from university to university. With science goes the technology created from the knowledge produced by research. Inevitably the spread of science with its associated technology makes toward uniformity in a multicultural world. This strain toward uniformity in cultures, when seen from the long view of history, has only begun. But great cultures and civilizations have their own peculiar genius. They resist change in core institutions, attitudes, and values. So the Japanese have put their own stamp on industrialism in the face of the similarity of its technology to industrial technology everywhere. In spite of the toughness of individual cultures, however, science opens new channels of discourse between peoples. The university, which includes the humanities along with science among its responsibilities, widens these channels. Whatever their particular tongue, university men and women speak a common language in the shop talk of their specialties. No matter in what country the university may be, the traveling scholar, when he sets foot on its grounds, feels at home. Universities over the world, sharing in the task of adding to a common body of knowledge and joining in the work of passing it on to generations of students, are moving toward what at some distant time may evolve into a new civilization. Already within the worldwide community of universities the vision of Socrates has validity for the scholar. "My country is the world," said the great Athenian. "My countrymen are all mankind."

Not only many cultures but many organized nation-states comprise the societal environment of the United States. These are power structures of varying strength and stability. Back of the present relationships of the great nations lies a long historical record of the coalescing and dissolution of power units, the aggrandizement, diminution, and conflicts of nations. In mid-twentieth century a great company of new and hopeful nations has appeared. Nationalism remains a primary force in the world. Over the globe men look to the nation-state as the chief instrument with which to effect their purposes. Changes in this societal environment have compelled changes in the United States.

World War II brought to maturity the concept and the practice of total war. Since 1945 total war has, in spite of the cessation of large-scale shooting, become continuous war. The appearance of the absolute weapon in the possession of the two greatest among the powers deflected the struggle to confrontations which did not threaten mutual massive destruction. Since World War II the

American people who, in the nineteenth century enjoyed an extraordinary sense of security, have had to learn to live with insecurity. A nation of tinkerers has made science the cornerstone of national defense. A people who in the nineteenth century maintained a small standing army primarily to police the sparsely settled frontier have given the military such budgetary support and such a place in the councils of the nation as the Founding Fathers never dreamed of. The foreseeable future offers no prospect of a lessening of the tension of the Cold War.

In the twentieth century, Americans were also forced to adjust to a new understanding of the limitations on national power, that of their own and of other nations. At the turn of the century Alfred Thayer Mahan had advanced and developed the concept of a fortress nation whose ramparts must be manned by an army and guarded from the sea by a navy. President Theodore Roosevelt went a long way in translating Mahan's theory into policy. He saw the great powers with whom he dealt as fortress-nations and locked to the fortifications of the Republic. The appearance in the mid-twentieth century of the nuclear bomb in the warhead of an intercontinental missile signified that the time had come when ramparts could be overflown. Moreover, the Nazi Fifth Columns in nations marked for conquest in World War II and the outward spread after the war of organized and skilled subversion from the power centers of communism demonstrated that national ramparts can be infiltrated. Mahan's once precise and persuasive concept became a period piece. The changed situation brought changed policies of government. The efforts to achieve a moratorium in nuclear testing, the lone American soldier ambushed and killed in Viet Nam, and the Internal Security Act of 1950 were all consequences of the obsolescence of national ramparts.

But nationalism did not go to the scrap heap. On the contrary it burgeoned. New, small and, for the most part, weak nation-states sprang up in Asia and Africa out of the ruins of once famous empires. At the same time the polarization of power between the two great land empires, the United States and the Soviet Union, became the primary fact in the international relations of the world. A logical consequence of the magnitude of the power possessed by these two giants appeared in a movement in Europe for smaller nations to coalesce into a power structure of comparable proportions. But in spite of logic, nationalism, French nationalism, interposed what seemed to be insuperable obstacles. The new African states met in conclave in Addis Ababa where they projected a dream of a united and powerful Africa. Then the delegates adjourned with pious words to resume the cultivation of the parochial nationalisms which, for the moment, they had laid aside.

What of the United States? National interest, of necessity, directed policy. Europe remained the front line for the forces defending the United States and in a nuclear world Washington kept the decision as to the use of the bomb. In the world arena the United States supported the United Nations, even to the point of making it into a limited power structure, primarily because so doing served the national interest. United Nations troops in the Congo made it possible for the Republic to avoid a confrontation with the Soviet Union in central Africa. Nationalism primarily determined the response of the United States to the conditions of the mid-twentieth-century world.

But the power brought into being by national needs brought commensurate responsibilities. Mid-twentieth-century Americans whose forefathers for generations had, for the most part, cultivated their gardens with small heed to peoples beyond their borders were compelled to reorient and enlarge their world view. They came to understand that they must take account of and do something about the grinding poverty of a terrifyingly large proportion of the world's population. Especially they became aware that history had made them not only the protagonists but the ultimate defenders of that tradition of humanism and freedom which had been the great achievement of Western civilization and the genius of their own culture. Almost from the time of their Revolution, Americans had

had a sense of mission. In the nineteenth century they thought of themselves as witnessing, before what they considered to be a monarchical and corrupt Europe, to the fact that free men could govern themselves. In the twentieth century the continuing and deadly challenge of a materialistic and totalitarian system made the mission crystal clear. The understanding of and the assumption of the responsibilities of power stands out as a major change in American life.

This change is closely linked to one which goes on within the borders of the nation. The Revolutionary Continental Congress spelled out in the eighteenth century the inalienable rights of men to life, liberty, and the pursuit of happiness; declared that government exists to protect and ensure these rights; and insisted that rule be by the consent of the governed. These values moved the men of 1776 to action. In the nearly two centuries since the Declaration, they provided the core values of a free and open society. They became measuring rods with which to assess political action. They brought about the extension of suffrage to all adult males in the first half of the nineteenth century and to women in the twentieth. They called into being the Emancipation Proclamation in 1863. Threatened by external dangers in World War I and World War II, they galvanized American men and women into action. Since these values were first proclaimed in 1776 they have functioned as the conscience of the American people and nation.

In the middle of the twentieth century the demands for change in social and political patterns are so far reaching as to approach, in certain communities of the nation, the dimensions of a social revolution. The Negro minority has called upon the core values of our society. These values have stirred that minority to the burdens and perils of nonviolent action. White Americans have recognized that the black minority strives to translate American ideals into social and political realities. The nation which understands its mission to be to defend freedomand human dignity against a ruthless totalitarianism struggles to make the dream of freedom and human dignity come true throughout its entire extent. The adversary is the most deep-seated prejudice known to mankind. In the present struggle for American civil rights within the United States, the Revolution of 1776 comes to its climax and the nation to a great test.

Evolving science and technology, shifting forces in the society of nations, and dynamism of old ideals and standards converge and synchronize to bring change to the life of twentieth-century Americans. The stirring and movement of no former age in our history can be compared with that of the middle decades of the twentieth century. Hurricane winds sweep across the American landscape. What the end will be only the future can disclose. But, as for the present, it is one of the supreme moments in history.

PART TWO

The two essays that follow were extracted from the chronology that has governed this selection because of their difference in length and density. With those that have preceded they share a central concern with the evolution of American values. Distinct from them, these two essays offer a comprehensive treatment of an aspect of the subject. The first reviews the course of American religious experience from the colonial origins to the time of writing, establishing a number of generalizations over and above the basic concern with value-derivation. The second and final essay is the most direct and extensive attack on the subject of values, limiting itself only by its emphasis on the traditional.

10

Religion in American Life

In our time America, born of Western Europe and now risen to power such as no nation ever before possessed, stands as the final bastion of the free world. Our civilization, harnessing the energy of the stars, moves forward like the progress of the whirlwind. Yet anxiety fills our thought. An attempt to scan the future ends only in frustration. Faced with a powerful, determined, and implacable enemy who challenges our nation, our values, and our religion, we suffer from a sense of insecurity.

Frustration and insecurity are, relatively speaking, novelties in our history. For brief times in our early national history we looked abroad with apprehension. But from 1815 to 1914 a sense of national security and security for our values and our religion provided the background for our thinking. World War I was a

SOURCE: Reprinted, with permission, from *National Policies for Education, Health and Social Services*, ed. James E. Russell (New York: Doubleday, 1955), Columbia University Bicentennial Series, p. 413-431. Copyright 1955 by the Trustees of Columbia University.

shock. The depression of the 1930s raised up apprehensions that led to vigorous constructive actions within the domestic scene. The fall of France in the summer of 1940 brought to Americans the sudden realization that an old and familiar world had disappeared and that the rising flood of a new war had washed away old defenses. Since the summer of Dunkirk Americans have felt insecure. Power and insecurity, the paradox of the mid-twentieth century, have gone together. Perhaps Americans, at long last, are learning to face the facts of life, namely, that the essence of life is hazard.

The rise of interest in religion stands out as one of the most conspicuous aspects of an age of anxiety. Evidence for this interest appears on every hand; the lists of best-selling books, the station coverage of religious television programs, the Sunday congregations in synagogues and churches. A conference on religion and education reflects the felt needs of the times.

A Heritage of Cultural Change

American civilization stems from the Middle Ages, the Reformation, and the Renaissance. American religious tradition began in the seventeenth century in that spiritual anxiety produced, in the words of Paul Tillich, "by the basic social conflict of the disintegrating Middle Ages." Out of this anxiety came some of our oldest and most important symbols: the Pilgrims, refugees for conscience' sake; William Penn, architect of a frontier settlement where men might be free to hear and to heed the inner voice; Roger Williams, wilderness prophet of religious freedom; the *Ark* and the *Dove*, bringing the men who established the medieval church on the shores of the Chesapeake. America came out of an age in which the struggle among the variant forms of religion evidenced the importance of religion itself for the men of those times.

But seventeenth-century England saw, along with the King

James translation of the Scriptures and the triumph of Cromwell, the culmination of what Herbert Butterfield has called the scientific revolution. As the first Americans enlarged their clearings and built their houses between the sea and the forest, Boyle brought forth chemistry out of alchemy; Harvey discovered the circulation of the blood; Newton, looking out into the heavens, mastered the mechanics of the solar system and discovered the laws of motion; and Locke, friend of Newton, grappled with the problems of the human understanding. In the following century, while colonial cities in America grew and the fringe of settlement moved westward, Enlightenment philosophy, a rationalism and humanism born of the triumphs of science and the philosophy of Locke, stirred Western thought including that of the English provinces in North America.

In 1803, as the nineteenth century opened, a Presbyterian clergyman in New York City, Samuel Miller, pointed out to his countrymen what he conceived to be the significance of seventeenth-century philosophy and science:

> At the close of the seventeenth century, the stupendous mind of Newton, and the penetrating genius of Locke, had laid their systems of matter and of mind before the world. Like pioneers in an arduous siege, they had many formidable obstacles to remove—many labyrinths to explore—and the power of numberless enemies to overcome. But they accomplished the mighty enterprise. With cautious, but firm and dauntless steps, they made their way to the entrenchments of fortified error; they scaled her walls; forced her confident and blustering champions to retreat; and planted the standard of truth, where the banner of ignorance and falsehood had so long waved.

Miller's phrases suggest the bright colors of what the eighteenth-century *philosophes* regarded as the Enlightenment dawn. But his words remind us of a basic fact in our tradition: That the history of our people in what is now the United States began in the age when modern science took form, and that history has moved forward in time, pacing evenly with the annals of creative scholarship in Western civilization.

Religion, however, rather than science, is the concern of this chapter. In 1947 in England a group of fourteen Anglicans of the "Catholic" school of thought, selected by the Archibishop of Canterbury "to examine the causes of the deadlock which occurs in discussion between Catholics and Protestants and to consider whether any synthesis between Catholicism and Protestantism is possible," reported to His Grace. Though some may quarrel with details of their analysis it may have uses for our present discussion. "The loss of 'wholeness' [the primitive unity of the early church]," the fourteen asserted, "became notorious and palpable with the schisms of the sixteenth century. . . . This separated Western tradition [which had long since moved away from the Eastern tradition] has in its turn broken down into three main types of Christianity with which the modern world is familiar: orthodox Protestantism, Liberalism, and post-Tridentine Catholicism. These three types are all represented in the Church of England [in the twentieth century]." Liberalism is a word whose edge is blunted with too much use. The fourteen defined Liberalism roughly as the spirit and tradition of the Renaissance. The post-Tridentine Roman Catholicism was based on the declarations of the Council of Trent (1564).

All three types exist in the religious faith of Americans in our day. But two of these, orthodox Protestantism and the Liberalism affected by the Renaissance impulse, provide the substance of the American religious tradition as it took form in our first two and a half centuries. The third, Roman Catholicism, though Lord Baltimore brought it to the Maryland colony in the early seventeenth century, was carried in the main to the United States after the close of the Napoleonic Wars as part of the mental baggage of migrating Europeans from many lands.

The fragmentation of the Christian tradition was a product of the energy and force of Western civilization, a culture already moving outward in the fifteenth century as Da Gama rounded the Cape of Good Hope and Columbus looked upon the strange men of the New World he had found. The horizons of Europeans had already begun to expand when, in 1517, Luther posted his theses on the door of the Wittenberg church. Two years after that event Magellan initiated the greatest maritime exploit in history, the circumnavigation of the globe.

American Adaptations

Energy and force characterized the American variant of Western culture from the seventeenth-century beginnings of the English colonies. The necessities of life on a remote frontier fostered activism. The circumstances of settlement that expressed the mind of capitalism more than of feudalism brought the individual into focus. Protestantism emphasized the relation of the individual to God. In the communities, strung like beads along the coast, men going about the tasks of daily living began to consider the relation of the individual to society.

Gradually, American colonials evolved a new conception of the relation of the individual to society. It was foreign to the Europe which was only beginning to move away from feudalism. The life story of Benjamin Franklin was only one among a multitude of American biographies that demonstrated the fact that, in the evolving and maturing colonies, the status and acceptance of the individual were not determined by his birth or place in a fixed class structure, but rather by his personal qualities and achievements. This New World pattern, not duplicated in either New France or

New Spain, represents what still remains the greatest American contribution to the social thought of the West.

To this achievement both the Reformation and the Renaissance contributed. Protestantism insisted that the individual, though he be the heir of corruption, must stand alone before his God. The fourteen Anglicans have defined the Renaissance impulse as it is used in this discussion:

> While the Reformation was proclaiming the helplessness of man, the "bondage of the will," the doctrine of Justification by Faith alone, the Renaissance was asserting its own idea of the dignity of man, and pointing toward the ideal of human freedom, and the idea of history as a steady progress of man toward happiness and enlightenment. Possessing roots both in ancient classical humanism and in the culture of the Western Church, the Renaissance had among its fruits many that could be called authentically Christian. The devotion to truth for its own sake, whether in the study of the Bible or in the discoveries of natural science, and the reverence for Man as created in the image of God—these insights are as necessary as is the Reformation insistence upon the priority of God's grace, or the Catholic insistence upon the visible Church.

The contributions of the Reformation and the Renaissance to the American philosophy of the relation of the individual to society sum up the most important contributions of religion to American life in the century and three-quarters of our colonial history.

The Puritan doctrine of determinism and of election, dividing men irrevocably into classes in terms of their destiny, ran athwart American social trends. It came out of a society in which a hierarchy of classes gave to every man his place. Seventeenth-century migrants to the colonies brought with them ideas of a hierarchy of classes to which life in England had conditioned them. But virtually none of the hereditary aristocracy crossed the sea, and the feudal arrangements that supported the gentry and nobility in the Old World gained only a small foothold in the American forest. Activism, required at first as a condition for survival and later continuing and developing as New England settlements achieved stability and prosperity, caused individuals to fall into natural divisions in accord with their merits. Colonial creativeness in building a civilization in a wilderness did not fit with the rigid determinism of the Calvinistic system or even with the covenant theology of Massachusetts Bay leaders. Perry Miller has described the intricate and sometimes tortuous reasoning by which late seventeenth-century New England theologians adapted a tough-minded theology to the movement of life along Massachusetts Bay and in the Connecticut valley. But the prudential ethics of the Puritans, which called upon men to be diligent and to deny themselves, suited perfectly a social scene in which the tasks were measured by the extent of the forest to be felled and where the hands to perform them were pitifully few.

The ideas of the Society of Friends accorded more closely with the movement of American life. Centering in Pennsylvania, the Friends spread from Rhode Island to Carolina. The Quakers emphasized liberty and established freedom of worship. They believed that God's voice may be heard in the hearts of the great and of the lowly, the learned and the unlettered. Out of this faith came a doctrine of man. The fact that the All Highest is willing to speak to and through the humble person gives him dignity and suggests the worth of a man. Quite logically, the Quaker ascribed dignity and worth to the stone-age Indian and to the laboring Negro slave. Men were needed in the colonies and were judged by their contributions to their communities. Colonials used only infrequently the harshest punishments of the Old World. The villages and the isolated clearings needed men so much that they could not bring themselves to execute thieves or to mutilate men guilty of crimes of violence. Though seventeenth-century Americans generally believed in witchcraft, its punishment, save for the tragedy at Salem, was light at a time when witch-burning had not yet disappeared from the Old World. Quaker doctrine reinforced and sanctified these attitudes growing up on the frontier.

The growing company that came after Roger Williams also developed articles of faith and a form of government both for church and state that supported in the eighteenth century the emerging American theory of the relation of the individual to society.

In the eighteenth century, the Renaissance impulse made itself felt as interest in science appeared in the faculties of colleges founded to train young men for service "in church and civil state," in particular at Harvard and Yale. Outside collegiate institutions a Quaker, John Bartram, in Pennsylvania achieved a reputation for his work in botany that extended to England. Oxford gave Franklin an honorary degree for his work in electricity. Along with science the Enlightenment emphasized liberty and humanism, teaching that the Author of Nature had endowed man with reason to the end that he might discover the laws laid down by the Author of the Universe and by so doing make progress through the generations toward the ultimate goal of perfection. Thomas Jefferson, using the language of the Enlightenment, wrote the American theory of the relation of the individual to society into the Declaration of Independence. This document proclaimed the inalienable right of every man to life, liberty, and the pursuit of happiness, the last a Jeffersonian phrase that meant the right of every man to make of himself what he can and to be accepted for what he is. If the Reformation and the Renaissance both contributed to this philosophy, it should be added that two resolute Catholics from the Chesapeake country, by setting their signatures to the Declaration, risked their lives in a struggle of uncertain outcome.

The Declaration of Independence, with the doctrine of natural rights as its core, has become the conscience of America. Today, wherever discrimination appears and equality of opportunity is denied, the Declaration of Independence pricks lethargic and sometimes reluctant men toward humaneness and justice.

Democracy and Religion

Winthrop S. Hudson, writing in 1953, has declared that a carefully defined equilibrium of church and state has been the great tradition of American religious and political life.

This great tradition, for such it is, should be viewed against its setting. In the final quarter of the eighteenth century Americans made decisions and spelled out accomplishments destined to bring a major turn to the course of history. They separated from the British Empire, thereby exorcising the institution of monarchy from their culture. Bristling language in the Constitution forbade an official aristocracy. The same Constitution created a political structure new to history, a Federal Republic resting on a popular foundation.

In this Republic, by the First Amendment, they forbade any national religious establishment. In a relatively short time thereafter, such preferential position as organized religion had in particular states disappeared. Freedom of religion, a pioneering American achievement, prevailed throughout the nation. In a day when, besides the family, the church and the state were the most important institutions in society, Americans made each the separate responsibility of the people. The event carried with it the implied affirmation that the state is not coterminous with society, as Burke, following the social contract theory, had affirmed. The generation of the Founding Fathers declared by their actions the conviction that life values are not subsumed wholly within either church or state but are divided between them. Americans at the turn of the nineteenth century made both political and ecclesiastical institutions dependent upon a free people.

Mr. Hudson has argued that pre-independence religious ideas

and practices contributed much to the decision. Religious freedom existed in Rhode Island and wherever the Quakers extended their influence they urged it. The natural rights theory, accepted by eighteenth-century Puritanism, implied it. The humanism and tolerance of the Enlightenment, emphasizing the pursuit of truth for its own sake, supported it. The multiplicity of religious organizations at the time required it. In America both the Reformation and the Renaissance contributed to what has become its great tradition. The building of the Federal Republic and the establishment of the principle of pluralism, as between church and state, together represent a peculiarly American creative achievement, building on the earlier formulation of a new relation between the individual and society.

In the crowded decades of the first half of the nineteenth century, the American version of expanding Western civilization produced a further achievement. Americans had required the years between 1607 and 1775, a period of more than a century and a half, to expand their settlements from the edge of the Atlantic to the Appalachians. In the following seventy-five years, they pushed west to the Pacific coast. The speed and magnitude of this conquest of the wilderness brought major problems to a growing people.

The leaders of the generation that founded the Republic understood two inevitable implications of making the state the responsibility of the people: the necessity that morals be maintained and the necessity that voters be literate and informed. Protestantism took up the former challenge. The rationalism of the Enlightenment fell into disrepute among Americans in the final decade of the eighteenth century as news of the bloody excesses of the French Revolution crossed the Atlantic. The Enlightenment had centered in France and had provided the background for the revolution. Tom Paine, who had once commanded a great audience, died early in the new century, after times and attitudes had changed, neglected and virtually ostracized. Timothy Dwight, president of Yale, looking across the ocean to the tumbrils of Paris, emphasized religion as the support of morals. Religion, said Dwight, exalts moral values and reminds the people of the moral law that comes from God. This grandson of Jonathan Edwards argued powerfully that because religion is the defender of morals it is the support of civilization, particularly in a self-governing republic where the people choose their rulers. If the people are lost in immorality, the state is lost and civilization is lost. ''Where religion prevails. . . ,'' thundered Dwight in 1798, ''a French Directory cannot govern, a nation cannot be made slaves, nor villains, nor atheists, nor beasts.''

In spite of the fact that the churches had always to contend with religious indifference on the part of many, Dwight's affirmation concerning religion expressed an axiom of nineteenth-century social thought. The sanctuary with its steeple pointing skyward provided in every community a material symbol for a fundamental conviction. Though, in the nineteenth century, Protestantism divided into multiplying denominations differing in ritual, organization, or creed, it preserved a remarkable unity in the matter of ethics. Puritanism and Quakerism had brought a prudential ethics, a worldly asceticism, to seventeenth-century America. Benjamin Franklin, though he did not accept the Puritan creed, had spread over the colonies, through the character of Poor Richard, the substance of Puritan prudential ethics. In the early nineteenth century the variously active Protestant sects carried to the expanding communities of the frontier the austere code that emphasized work, sobriety, self-restraint, and the renouncing of frivolity. In an age when westward-moving Americans improvised governments in territory after territory, orthodox Protestantism gave to new communities the moral discipline that made self-government possible. In frontier communities disfigured by the chicane of the land speculator, by the brawls of the saloon, and by the violence of thieves and bandits, the churches, often planted as missions by the men of the East, provided centers to which pioneer families who valued decency and decorum could rally.

In both East and West in the first half of the nineteenth century, moreover, Protestantism ignited spirits such as those of Dorothea Dix, Lyman Beecher, and Theodore Weld. Humanitarian movements—the betterment of the lot of the mentally ill, the provision of opportunities for education for deaf children, the battle against alcoholism—attacked the evils of the day and sought to ameliorate the suffering and enlarge the opportunities of the unfortunate and the oppressed. This story, whose climax was the antislavery crusade, needs no retelling. The humanitarian urge did not, however, stem wholly from the Reformation. The humanism of the Renaissance also contributed. Religious liberals—William Ellery Channing, Theodore Parker, Ralph Waldo Emerson, Henry David Thoreau—attacked the evils of emerging industrialism and warred against chattel slavery. Abraham Lincoln, intellectual descendant of the Enlightenment, became the emancipator of the slave.

But religion had its failures in the first half of the nineteenth century along with its successes. Emerson drove over from Concord to Cambridge one day in 1837 to address the assembled members of the Harvard Phi Beta Kappa society. He spoke frankly, almost sharply, to the young men. "He who would be a man," said Emerson, "must be a non-conformist." James Fenimore Cooper had anticipated Concord's first citizen. The creator of Leatherstocking had told his fellow countrymen in an unpopular book in the 1830s that the arrogant assertion of majority opinion in the United States threatened American individualism. Let the majority be content, said Cooper in effect, when it has enacted its will into law. Americans should permit unpopular ideas and causes to have a chance. Cooper pointed to the easy resort to violence that characterized the period in both East and West. Turbulence marred the 1830s and 1840s. Mobs recruited from the Protestant majority attacked the Catholics, whose immigration increased after 1815. In the 1830s, when Garrisonian abolition of slavery was a dangerous radicalism, a mob dragged Garrison through Boston streets with a rope about his body and another mob in Illinois shot the abolitionist Lovejoy to death. One paid a price for nonconformity. On June 10, 1844, a crowd gathered in the village of Carthage in Illinois and moved through the main street to the stone jail. Forcing their way in, they shot and killed two brothers. One of the two was called by his followers a prophet. These followers had already been harried from place to place by hostile communities about them. Now in Nauvoo on the Mississippi they gathered, after the lynching, what possessions they could salvage and began the long trek across the plains. In Utah an unflagging faith and the discipline of an authoritarian church enabled these latter-day refugees for conscience' sake to subdue and civilize a desert. Now in the twentieth century a million believers revere the memory of the martyred prophet. They still read in their sacred writings words they believe he had from God: "Fear not, little flock. The kingdom is yours until I come. Behold, I come quickly." The nineteenth-century persecutions of the Catholics and the Mormons are also part of American religious tradition.

The events of the age demonstrated that to make religion the responsibility of the people was to subject its practice to such hazards inherent in democracy as the tyranny of the majority illustrated above. The warnings of Emerson and Cooper, both in the liberal religious tradition, against the forces making in the 1830s for conformity provide a background for similar problems arising a little more than a century later.

The men of the 1830s and 1840s, however, did not despair of democracy. Rather, they moved decisively to develop it. In these decades they completed the process of the elimination of property qualifications from voting and in nearly all the states extended the suffrage to all white male citizens. In America the age of the common man began in Jackson's time.

An American democratic faith took form. Three doctrines of this faith made a kind of triad. (1) The age affirmed a fundamental law underlying society and making it possible, a law including the idea of natural rights and the religious moral code expressed in the ten commandments of the Old Testament and in the New Testament double-love commandment. Emerson insisted that morality is the very heart of the universe, for morality is the very essence of the immanent and all-pervading Over-Soul. (2) To this general idea of a fundamental law men added the doctrine of the free individual, responsible for his conduct before the law and equal with his fellows in the rights and obligations arising from it. (3) Finally, the times fostered a doctrine of mission, the mission of America, born of a struggle for liberty, to stand before the world as a witness that common men can rule themselves without the aid of hereditary aristocrats or princes.

From the Reformation came the moral overtones of this democratic faith; from the Renaissance its emphasis on liberty and on the ability of man. Confidence in progress, the advance to better things, gave a certain *élan* to this faith of the early nineteenth century. Americans assumed that, one day, life-giving democracy would spread over the world. But they assumed also that it would go in partnership with Christianity. The American democratic faith matured in a period when American Christians, particularly in the older states, turned their thoughts outward and established missions on distant and little-known continents. An oration delivered in Kentucky on July 4, 1843, suggests the blending of Christian and democratic hope characteristic of the time. ''Christianity, rational philosophy, and constitutional liberty,'' said George Robertson of the Kentucky bench, ''like an ocean of light are rolling their resistless tide over the earth.''

Education Fostered by Church and State

At home, meanwhile, Americans came to grips with another problem that must be solved if free government was to endure. James Madison had once warned that, if popular government were not to be the prelude to a farce or a tragedy, it must rest on an educated citizenry. The citizens of the Republic, responsible in the Great Tradition for both church and state, gave thought to education.

The tradition of higher education ran back to Harvard in the early seventeenth century. The religious drive of the Reformation had called the first American colleges into being. But, as has already been noted, the attitudes and the goals of the Renaissance made their impress soon after the eighteenth century opened. At the end of that century Timothy Dwight, president of Yale, sent a young man, Benjamin Silliman, to Britain to master the natural science of the time and to return to establish it at New Haven.

In the nineteenth century, though universities founded by the states appeared, Americans used organized religion to scatter colleges over the West and South. Too often the creation of these institutions reflected the urge of denominational rivalry. But the higher motive was to bring the light of knowledge to the expanding communities of a simple agricultural-commercial civilization, in the conviction that the treasures of learning ennoble life as does the inspiration of faith. In these independent colleges the chapel bell called faculty and students to prayers before they turned to Euclid or to Livy. Williams College in western Massachusetts reflected the common primacy of religion in the partnership. "What is education," wrote President Mark Hopkins to one of his trustees in 1851, "if it does not lead the mind to its true good? How much better to be a ploughboy and a Christian, than to be a vicious, sensual, conceited collegian!"

At the same time the generation that used organized religion for the founding of most of the institutions of higher learning chose the political state as the instrument for the establishment of the public school. In an age when, in the Old World, social class determined the nature and even the possibility of education for the individual, Americans, guided by their democratic faith, formulated the goal of education for all. They made education the instrument for giving reality to the ideal of equality of opportunity. Taking account of the magnitude of the problem of providing schooling for the children of a people spreading swiftly over a country as large as Europe, they concluded that their voluntary religious associations were inadequate to the task. The basic assumptions of the Judeo-Christian tradition embedded in the democratic faith of the time provided the background for the multiplying schools. The moral precepts in the ubiquitous schoolbooks of Noah Webster and McGuffey carried to the desks of the pupils the spirit and outlook of the age.

Three men associated with the tragedy of the Civil War suggest in their lives that spirit and that outlook. On July 4, 1861, the Congress assembled at the call of President Lincoln. The day marked the eighty-fifth anniversary of the Declaration of Independence. Sumter had fallen and war had blazed in the border states. The President addressed to the Congress a message setting forth his policy for the preservation of the Union. "And having chosen our course without guile and with pure purpose," concluded Lincoln, "let us renew our trust in God, and go forward without fear, and with manly hearts."

Across the battle lines two men, bound together in close association, emerged to personify the Confederate will to independence. Robert E. Lee, burdened with heavy responsibility, prayed frankly for victory and did not permit failure to shake his faith. "I had taken every precaution," he remarked of an operation in Virginia, "to insure success and had counted on it. But the Ruler of the Universe willed it otherwise and sent a storm to disconcert a well-laid plan and to destroy my hopes." Dependence upon a power greater than man gave Lee the poise that enabled him to remain the leader of his people after his army and his nation had crumbled into dust. Stonewall Jackson, Lee's great lieutenant, held fast to the stern faith of the Puritans. He made duty his religion. On an active campaign and in independent command, Jackson made his way one evening to the bivouac of his old brigade to attend a prayer meeting. His youngest staff officer went with him and later left a record of the scene. "The camp was there. Bowed heads, bent knees, hats off, silence! Stonewall Jackson was kneeling to the Lord of Hosts in prayer for his people. Not a sound disturbed his voice as it ascended to heaven in their behalf. . . . When he left, a line of soldiers followed him in escort to the edge of the camp."

The Second Inaugural—"With malice toward none, with charity for all, with firmness in the right as God gives us to see the right"—one of the finest expressions of religious faith and purpose in our literature, stood out in the waning conflict and marked the end of an age. Whatever else may be said about the old religion—and its shortcomings were many—pride was not its besetting sin. Jackson, Lee, and Lincoln looked up humbly toward their God.

The Acceleration of Cultural Change

I have dealt with origins. In our day when an American colossus musters vast power, Thoreau's building a hut on Walden Pond seems long ago, as does the simple life of most Americans of that time—though not simple enough for him. We had vigor then as a people. Our present power did not just happen. It was developing with each generation. It represents the creativeness of Western civilization. Two major wars slowed and hampered the creativeness of Europe. The United States, spared the invader's trail of wreckage, carried on with accelerating speed.

No less than five revolutions have intervened between Lincoln's day and our own. (1) Economic enterprise has created a mechanized industrial civilization of surpassing productive capacity. (2) Between the Civil War and World War I a river of immigrants, principally from Europe, modified the ethnic character of our people. (3) Industrialization brought urbanization and immigrants swelled the population of the metropolitan centers. (4) Faced with the insecurities for the individual rising from a complex and highly mechanized economy, Americans were driven to action by the disaster of the depression, magnified the political state, and learned to use big government for purposes of social engineering. (5) Meanwhile, out of the college of Mark Hopkins' day Americans had created the modern university, the best examples of which have taken their places beside those ancient centers of learning that have given Western civlization much of its quality and character.

New Learning

Of the five great cultural changes since Appomattox, the emergence of the university and the laboratory was basic. Civilization rests on a body of knowledge. The prime reason for the differences between the New England of Jonathan Edwards and that of our own day may be found in the differences in the sum of knowledge available for men to draw on to meet the needs of life. The growth of the natural sciences in Europe and in the United States made possible the evolving technology that released the energy and created the machines of a mechanized age.

As Americans in 1865 turned away from their four years' preoccupation with fratricidal war, they found themselves facing a new and strange cosmos. The natural philosophy of Benjamin Silliman's day had supplemented rather than conflicted with religious ideas, though geology had stirred apprehensions among those who interpreted the Scriptures literally. Darwin, coming into American consciousness principally after the Civil War, had proposed a revolutionary alteration in the accepted concept of the origin of man. For many Americans the old vision of a friendly universe presided over by a deity who had created man a little lower than the angels and was mindful of the fall of the sparrow in the field began to dissolve. Mark Twain, casting off the Calvinism with which his childhood had been burdened, tried to reconcile his natural generosity and humanity with a dour philosophy that man comes out of nature and that a remorseless chain of cause and effect drives nature on—no one knows whither or why. He failed to make the reconciliation, but the philosophy seized and held him, bringing black pessimism to his later years. Thousands of Twain's contemporaries, sensing the threat of the new, developing science to old intellectual securities, held fast desperately to familiar certitudes. In America in the second half of the nineteenth century, the Renaissance and the Reformation clashed. The story of the beginning of Cornell University illuminates the meaning of what was happening.

In 1867 Ezra Cornell and Andrew D. White founded the university that overlooks Lake Cayuga. "Our purpose," said White later, "was to establish an institution for advanced instruction and research, in which science, pure and applied, should have an equal place with literature. . . . We had specially determined that the institution should be under the control of no political party and of no single religious sect. . . . It certainly never entered into the mind of either of us that we were doing anything irreligious or unChristian. . . . As I look back across the intervening years, I know not whether to be more astonished or amused at our simplicity. Opposition began at once. In the Legislature it confronted us at every turn, and it was soon in full blaze throughout the State—from the good Protestant bishop who proclaimed that all professors should be in holy orders, since the Church alone was given the command, 'Go teach all nations,' to the zealous priest who published the charge that Goldwin Smith—a profoundly Christian scholar—had come to Cornell (from England) to inculcate infidelity." White fought back. In an address at Cooper Institute a little later he fired the first gun of a long campaign. "In all history," declared the Cornell president, "interference with science in the name of religion, no matter how conscientious such interference may have been, has resulted in the direct evils both to religion and science. . . and all untrammeled scientific investigation, no matter how dangerous to religion some of its stages have seemed to be, has invariably resulted in the highest good for both religion and science."

Long before Cornell was founded, the state university had appeared, a development that gained new impetus with the passage of the Morrill Land Grant Act in 1862. New universities established after the middle of the nineteenth century on foundations that were independent of the state were, for the most part, free from ecclesiastical control. Church-connected older universities that had not already done so tended to move toward a similar freedom. Many of the smaller liberal arts colleges that grew out of the religious drives of the nineteenth century, however, held fast to old and basic ties.

If orthodox Protestantism had its ethical code, so also did scholarship. White embarked upon a crusade to make the citizens of New York State understand the meaning and significance of the principles that govern scholarship. The scholar's code follows: To break out from the confines of ignorance into the light of new knowledge, the investigator must be free to follow the trail toward enlightenment wherever it may lead. He must be honest and sometimes courageous in recording and reporting what he finds while on his search. If he falsifies, if he warps his report to creed or party line, he makes no addition to knowledge; he only wastes his time. He must make use of the clues and knowledge gleaned by other men who took the trail before him. He must trust them and must, in turn, be worthy of the trust of his contemporaries and successors for the conquest of new knowledge is a cooperative undertaking. In order to save the truth he comes to comprehend and to profit by, the investigator must give it away, following the example of those who have gone before him.

This code, the expression of the Renaissance impulse, is absolute. The totalitarian chieftain may press his men of science into the service of the state; but, if he would have them add to the sum of knowledge, he must mark out and protect an area in which they may be intellectually free. The code is the fundamental law of

creative intellectual life. It undergirds the technological civilization in which we live. It became ideal and guide to the companies
of scholars comprised by the rising universities. No element in the
code denied the ethics or the faith of religion. Scholars labored in a
particular and limited field in the quest for truth. But within that
field they insisted upon the primacy of the principles upon which
they founded their work.

New Theology

After Appomattox one wing of Protestantism held fast to traditional positions as conflicts arose out of science and out of historical investigation; another attempted to understand the significance, for the faith, of the emerging body of knowledge. These
latter men in the final decades of the nineteenth century, accepting
the insights of the Renaissance, tried to bring them into the service
of the Reformation. They attempted the formulation of a "new
theology." Their ideal was essentially the same as that announced
in 1953 by an American Catholic scholar, discussing possible
standards and guides for action for his church. "Another standard
for Catholic life and education," wrote Julian Pleasants, "is the
revelation of God, not only Revelation with a capital 'R' but
revelation with a small 'r': the revelation of the Artist which we
find in His Art, the revelation of the Lawmaker which we find in
His laws, the revelation of the Planner's intentions which we find
in the way He has made things."

The Protestant creators of the New Theology fell short of greatness. They were sometimes bewildered, as were their contemporaries, including the growing company of scholars in the universities, by the surge and drive of American life as our people hurried
into the unfamiliar age of power and technology. Those who
shaped and those who accepted the New Theology have been
charged with accepting the world. They did, if Lyman Abbott's
forceful affirmation that religion must not interfere with the free-

dom of the investigator is called surrender to the world. They have been called complacent acceptors of the status quo. Yet in their day the social gospel, successor to the humanitarianism of antebellum days, took form to stir the consciences of Christians to the end that sufferers from the evils of unregulated capitalism and a burgeoning urbanism be given aid and protection. If Washington Gladden and Walter Rauschenbusch stood first among the Protestants who faced and sought to deal with the hard facts of their time, they led a considerable muster.

The men of the New Theology (to become liberal Protestantism or Modernism) shared the mind and outlook of their age. The generation that saw the century turn took progress for granted. The conquest of ''yellow jack'' in Cuba and the escape of earth-bound man into the air at Kitty Hawk stretched the imaginations of those who looked to the future. Historians call the period the Progressive Era because ''progress'' became its key word. Looking backward the men of the time saw that from its beginning America had moved forward. Evils had been imported or had arisen, with chattel slavery the blackest of all. Americans had struck slavery down. They would strike down the evils of a new day. The social criticisms in the social gospel did not conflict with the belief that the nation marched toward better things. Criticism implemented progress. Protestant men and women shared in the *élan* of a swiftly moving time. The Student Volunteer Movement, originating on the eve of the Progressive Era, announced a hope and goal that could only have been accepted in such a time of hope and confidence, namely, ''the evangelization of the world of this generation.'' Christian doctors and teachers as well as preachers set out in significant numbers to make the vision a reality.

Granted that, when judged by the wisdom of hindsight, the Americans of the period, both those who prized religion and those who were indifferent, were naive. At least, when judged by the light they possessed, they achieved pertinent criticism, initiated significant reforms, and cultivated a generous sympathy. There existed a relationship, not yet fully explored, between the concern of the social gospel and the reform or "progressive movement" in political life. If the era ended in disaster, tragedy came because Europe collapsed into war. The true twentieth century, the century of violence and revolution, began with a shot fired at Sarajevo. Three years later, in 1917, Americans still not comprehending, still generous, believed the phrases of President Wilson to be genuine possibilities for the future: make the world safe for democracy, the war to end war. American Protestantism, like other churches, because their people were Americans conditioned by their age, supported the Great Crusade.

Americans were closer to Europe in 1914 than they had been in Emerson's day, though that fact had little to do with their entry into the war. Immigrants had completed the ethnic revolution that had begun with the close of the Napoleonic Wars. New men and women spoke strange languages in American streets and brought with them memories of peasant villages or of crowded cities from places as far away as Sicily, Greece, Armenia, and the Ukraine. They brought with them Old World religions: Roman Catholicism, holding fast to the essential doctrines of the medieval church; the Eastern Orthodox communion; Judaism, looking to Abraham and to Moses for inspiration. Different religions provided consolation and a cultural focus for different groups of impoverished and confused strangers trying to find their places in a hustling civilization.

Because Irishmen came early and in large numbers, they assumed leadership among the Roman Catholics. But, where in time Poles, Italians, and French Canadians concentrated in sufficient numbers, the priest who spoke their tongue and the sanctuary where they worshipped helped them to find their own identity as a group of similar people and by so doing eased for them the hard transition from Old World living to the strange ways of the New. The rabbi and the synagogue, the Roman Catholic priest and his church, and the sanctuaries of the Orthodox church performed similar services for their congregations. Immigration brought the newer minorities into being and these newer Americans found, with relatively few exceptions, fundamental life values in religion. An older minority, the Negro who had been in America since 1619, now freed from chattel slavery, found in his own Protestant churches places of refuge where his spirit could be free and where his prayers and songs could express without restraint his sentiments, his longings, and his faith: "Nobody Knows the Trouble I've Seen," "Were You There When They Crucified My Lord?," "Little Boy, How Old Are You?" Outside their churches, in the phrase of Paul Lawrence Dunbar, they wore the mask.

Religion in Modern Culture

"Religion is not in a robust state of health in modern civilization," declared Reinhold Niebuhr in 1927. "Vast multitudes, particularly in industrial and urban centers, live without seeking its sanctions for their actions and die without claiming its comforts in their extremities. The sickness of faith in our day may be the senility which precedes death; on the other hand, it may be a specific malady which thought and time can cure. If history is slow to destroy that which has become useless, it may be as patient and persistent in reviving what is useful but seems dead."

Niebuhr was not alone in his pessimism. Hornell Hart wrote the report on Attitudes in *Recent Social Trends*, a study initiated by President Hoover and published in 1933. Some headings in the report indicate the nature of the material that Hart's investigation turned up: "Decline in the Proportion of Books on Religion," "Decline in the Proportion of Articles on Religion," "The Bible Receives Less than Half the Attention It Had Twenty-Five Years Ago," "Declining Approval of Organized Christianity." The report, however, was not wholly negative. "While traditional Christianity," said Hart, "has been sinking to a new low point in public interest and esteem . . . certain religious topics and concepts have in recent years reached new high levels of attention. . . . In general it may be said that the topics which have shown smallest losses of attention, or which have shown net gains, have been related to aspects not in direct conflict with science and not enmeshed in ecclesiasticism, but based on personal experience and involving applications of the 'social gospel' to economic problems.''

Certain trends in the times provide a background for the religious situation reported. Disillusionment came to Americans in the 1920s. The peace did not make the world safe for democracy. The war to end war seemed to have done little more than reorient the old power struggle among the nations. The fine idealism of 1917-18 seemed in retrospect romantic dreaming. Churchmen who in 1917 had thought of themselves as participating in and sanctifying a great crusade began to suspect that they had been dupes. In company with Harry Emerson Fosdick many Protestant ministers determined that never again would they support the devilish institution of war. Among the educated public, idealism in many circles fell into disrepute, interesting primarily as reflecting the mental stature of well-intentioned but soft-headed ''do-gooders.''

At the same time, the upsurge of Fundamentalism with its militant anti-intellectualism astounded the educated citizenry that thought the questions raised by Darwin three-quarters of a century before had largely been settled. Moreover, in its efforts to meet the Fundamentalist attack, Modernism seemed to lack assurance and power. The year of the Dayton trial extravaganza saw the Ku Klux Klan reach its peak. Two years later the execution of Sacco and Vanzetti climaxed a postwar chapter of fear and of hostility toward the radical foreigner who threatened the basic institutions of our country. The 1920s was the decade of isolationism. It was the decade of Lewis, Fitzgerald, Dreiser, Mencken, and the emerging Hemingway. It was the decade of revolutions brought about by the mass acceptance of the motor car and the radio.

The fourteen Anglicans who reported to the Archbishop of Canterbury in 1947 offered a comment that has pertinence to the American scene in the 1920s: "But these Renaissance insights [the devotion to truth for its own sake, whether in the study of the Bible or in the discoveries of science, and the reverence for man as created in the image of God] have, through their isolation from other insights into man's relation to God, led the way to some of the tragedies of modern secularism and godlessness. . . . The belief that man is created in God's image can turn into a belief in man as man. . . . The belief that there is a real connection between the Christian faith on the one hand, and culture, education, social betterment, and human emancipation on the other, can degenerate into the belief that God's kingdom is wholly within history, and may be identified with human progress."

The naturalism that Mark Twain had accepted flourished in the literature and the literary criticism of the 1920s and 1930s. Robert Frost, with a wry smile, commented on the age:

> Our worship, humor, conscientiousness
> Went long since to the dogs under the table.
> And served us right for having instituted
> Downward comparisons. As long on earth
> As our comparisons were stoutly upward
> With gods and angels, we were men at least,
> But little lower than the gods and angels.
> But once comparisons were yielded downward,
> Once we began to see our images
> Reflected in the mud and even dust,
> 'Twas disillusion upon disillusion.
> We were lost piecemeal to the animals,
> Like people thrown out to delay the wolves.
> Nothing but fallibility was left us . . .

The poet from north of Boston was a little hard on the age.

Naturalism in America in the 1920s and again in the 1930s, as it expressed itself in literature and in legal and political theory, never lost sight of the worth of man or the importance of striving for a better life. The swiftly growing social sciences, resting on naturalist assumptions, sought to add to the sum of knowledge concerning man and society to the end that man might meet more intelligently the conditions of life. With few exceptions naturalism in the United States was associated with meliorism. In America no party leader or head of state arose, as in Germany, to propose and attempt a literal and ruthless application of the concept of the survival of the fittest through the mass extermination of unwanted populations. In America the life of reason had developed a world view with a humanistic core, a view and outlook that occupied a place beside conventional religion and that generated aspiration and stimulated loyalty to human values.

Niebuhr in 1927 concluded his estimate of the plight of religion in the United States as of that year: "A psychology of defeat," he commented, "of which both fundamentalism and modernism are symptoms has gripped the forces of religion. . . . To retreat from untenable positions is no doubt a necessary step in preparation for new advances; but this necessary strategy has not been accompanied by the kind of spiritual vigor which would promise ultimate victory. The general tendencies toward secularization of life have been consistent enough to prompt its foes to predict religion's ultimate extinction as a major interest of mankind and to tempt even friendly observers to regard its future with grave apprehension."

But the century of revolution and violence that began with World War I came to a climax in what has been called an "Age of Anxiety." Anxiety transformed the place of religion in American culture. The tumultuous events of the 1940s provided cumulative illustration of the old truism that knowledge is power. It was power indeed when it created the atom bomb. But there were other manifestations. "Science," remarked Lawrence Dennis in 1940, "has given the experts more skill, knowledge, and instruments for manipulating the masses than the medicine men and witch doctors of old ever commanded.'' Twentieth-century men faced the paradox that, if addition to the sum of knowledge can be achieved only through obedience to an absolute ethical code, the knowledge thus won and the power it gives are neutral and may be used for good or evil ends. The paradox was compounded, moreover, by the fact that power bred fear; fear required secrecy as a divided world moved into an armaments race; and secrecy, compelled by the needs of national survival, set barriers across that free interchange of discoveries that is the lifeblood of science. Perhaps the pursuit of knowledge had by its very triumphs planted the seeds of decay in the heart of scientific civilization.

Power won by reason had, moreover, created a situation that compelled mid-twentieth-century man, the American included, to face the possibility of either suffering or inflicting mass destruction. Looking back on their recent history, Americans, while they recognized the purpose and the result of saving lives of thousands of American soldiers set for the landing on the mainland of Japan in 1945, noted that it is part of the record of history that the greatest democracy in the world pioneered in the creation and the use of the most terrible weapon known to man. In 1950, after the President had announced the decision to push ahead with the creation of an H-bomb, twelve nuclear physicists including Hans A. Bethe, formerly director of Theoretical Physics at the Los Alamos Laboratories, proposed that the United States make a solemn pledge not to be the first to use the prospective weapon. ''We believe,'' said the twelve, ''that no nation has the right to use such a bomb, no matter how righteous its cause. This bomb is no longer a weapon of war but a means of extermination of whole populations. Its use would be a betrayal of all standards of morality and of Christian civilization itself.''

Americans in the midcentury have found themselves caught in a cruel dilemma. They faced an implacable foe, armed also with the absolute weapon, who challenged not only their nation but their democratic and religious faith. To meet this threat necessity compelled them to contemplate the possible use of a weapon of horror beyond the capacity of the imagination to encompass. To curb and discipline power, therefore, became the first need of the age. Faced with this need, Americans, as never before in their history, turned to explore the realm of the spirit for help and hope. Perhaps the need to hold power in check was merely a corollary to another need. Some thought so.

"The perils that confront man today," remarked Edmund Sinnott, biologist, in 1953, "come from the fundamental difference between his spiritual insight and his rational power in the deep problems he has to face. This difference is dramatized by the divergent attitudes of those two great disciplines, science and religion, with which he tries to comprehend the universe. . . . We should not regret these differences between the discipline of reason and of spirit but rather rejoice in them. They are two halves that make man whole. From tension between them character is born. Perhaps in us is being fought a skirmish in the great battle of the universe. Man, half ape and half angel, half matter and half spirit, has a place within each world. Herein lies his glory, his tragedy, and the possibility for him of tremendous things."

11

Traditional Values in American Life

Declaration of Faith

"I have never had a feeling politically that did not spring from the Declaration of Independence. . . . I have often inquired of myself what great principle it was that kept this confederacy so long together. It was not the mere matter of separation of the colonies from the motherland, but something in that declaration giving liberty, not alone to the people of this country, but hope for the world for all future time. It was that which gave promise that in due time the weights would be lifted from the shoulders of all men, that all should have an equal chance. This was the sentiment embodied

SOURCE: This paper was written at the request of and for the United States National Commission for UNESCO. It served as the American contribution to a dialogue with India dealing with the traditional values of the two nations. The Indian National Commission for UNESCO produced a paper of similar character. The American paper was published in 1960 by the Government Printing Office.

148

in the Declaration of Independence. . . . I would rather be assassinated on the spot than surrender it.''

President-elect ABRAHAM LINCOLN
February 22, 1861
Independence Hall in Philadelphia

Every society creates ideal images of what the behavior in thought and action of its members should be. When taken together, these images express the vision of the good life that the people of the society have achieved. These images, known and approved by the members of the society, give form to its values. A value is an ideal, a paradigm setting forth a desired and esteemed possible social reality. In essence, values are beliefs—beliefs that the idealized ways of living and acting are the best ways for the society. Because values are beliefs, they serve to inspire the members of the society to act in the approved ways. Because values are ideal pictures, they provide a means of judging the quality of actual behavior. In this role they become standards.

Values vary in importance. Standards of good manners do not have the same rank in the hierarchy of values as those of the basic ethical code of the society. Custom regulates manners. Formal laws sanction much of the ethical code. As civilizations evolve in the processes of history, values change. Each generation combines the tradition it has inherited from the past with the knowledge that springs from an experienced present to formulate and reformulate the values which guide the conduct of its members. Because in the sense just mentioned values are always in the process of reformulation, advanced societies subject them to continuous rational criticism. Institutions, such as the family and the school, continually transmit values to oncoming generations. Other institutions, in particular those of religion, exhort and encourage the members of a society to make their behavior conform to its picture of the good life.

An illustration may illuminate the nature of values. Citizens of the United States esteem individual liberty. They value liberty because they believe that maximum freedom within bounds set by the general welfare enables the individual person to express more fully the qualities and powers within him and, as a consequence, to live with the dignity that springs from the ability to make his own choices and the opportunity to achieve such ends as his capacities permit. Nature, however, sets limits to human behavior. Society must establish others because individual liberty, when carried to the extreme, becomes anarchy. Besides individual liberty, our people esteem the authority of law—law that is made in their name by their elected representatives. Our citizens believe that only in the context of social order maintained by law can the individual person live a full and significant life. Particular values, then, may stand opposed to one another, as the opposition just noted and recognized since the time of the ancient Greeks between liberty and authority. Americans, as other people have done, have brought these opposing values into balance in the combined ideal and standard of liberty under law.

An overall view of the civilizations (or cultures) of the world discloses that today, as in the past, behavior esteemed in one culture may be disapproved in another. The discovery and exploration of this ethical relativity among the various peoples of the world is one of the more important achievements of the science of cultural anthropology in the twentieth century. This knowledge that standards of value and codes of morality vary over the world conditions the anthropologist when he seeks to understand the ways of a people strange to him. The knowledge of cultural relativity compels on his part an open-minded approach. He tries to avoid judgments on the behavior of the people he is studying that are based on the standards and values of the cultures from which the investigator comes. As a scientist, the anthropologist approaches the strange society neither to praise nor to blame, but to understand. But improved transportation and communication have so shrunk the world that peoples once distant from one another have been brought close together. All thinking men of whatever country must in our time take up the inquiry of the anthropologist. The conditions of the world require that the peoples try earnestly to understand one another's ways.

Anthropology brought forth the hypothesis of ethical relativity in a century of tensions and violence. As the decades passed, however, the theory seemed to an increasing number of persons to fail to probe to the depths of life. The mid-twentieth-century generations saw and experienced in more than one culture conspicuous evil acts, too dark to be justified and therefore condemned throughout the world. Out of the spiritual wellsprings of their beings came the conviction that in human affairs some forms of behavior are always wrong. The Declaration of Human Rights drawn up under the sponsorship of the United Nations was a preliminary reconnaissance in the region of universal values.

The present essay attempts an outline of the values of one civilization, that of the United States. The basic documents of our national culture—the Declaration of Independence and the Constitution, the latter written in 1787 and amended more than a score of times as a result of growing knowledge and evolving understandings—provide the starting points for this study of our values. The laws of the land as interpreted by the courts through more than a century and a half offer additional material. The historical record presents the annals of achievement and of failure on the part of the people of the nation to measure up to the high standards of their ideals. The values discussed in the following pages are those more important ideals which seem to the present investigator to have been and to be accepted by the great majority of our citizens. He has submitted his findings to many critics in many walks of life and has profited by a very large number of suggestions. But the essay must remain a personal appraisal. In considering it, the non-American must remember that a basic characteristic of our culture is the fact that the citizens of the

United States, when taken collectively, assert in freedom a diversity of opinions.

This essay sets forth an outline that, when put beside similar statements from other civilizations, will, it is hoped, provide a springboard for a comparative exploration. Out of such an enterprise can come a greater depth of cross-cultural understanding and an enlargement of mutual understanding through awareness of the beliefs as to what constitutes the good life held by peoples who are neighbors on our planet. Perhaps comparisons and discussions may bring a little more clearly into view the shape of those universal values which our awareness of the evil in human life and our knowledge of the capacity for nobility of the human heart compel us to believe exist for the guidance of men.

The Tradition Out of Which
American Values Have Come

The values that Americans cherish emerge from a tradition that originated in the ancient Middle East and in ancient Greece and Rome. At that time other great and old civilizations flourished in China and India. Inevitably, cultural interchange and borrowing took place among the peoples living in those far distant centuries. The Indo-European languages spreading in very early times to the South and to the West established subtle similarities over large areas of Asia and Europe. But Greece, Rome, and the Middle East provided the specific places of origin of the civilization we call Western that has evolved now for 2,500 years on the continent of Europe. Different peoples, such as the French, the Spaniards, the Danes, and the English, developed their own peculiar variants of what became in its turn one of the world's great civilizations. In the eighteenth, nineteenth, and twentieth centuries, the people of the United States created their particular variant of this civilization. Because of the common heritage of Western culture, the values of

Americans derive ultimately from the same sources as do those of Europeans. The mind of the West has evolved from the Judeo-Christian faith of the ancient Middle East and from the science, philosophy, and art of classical Greece, together with the law of Rome.

The ancient Middle East gave to the West a monotheistic religion from which came two formulations of basic importance for Western (including American) thought:

1. The idea of the importance of the individual soul in the eyes of God.
2. The idea that Deity not only approves righteous behavior but has laid down a moral law to govern the relations of men in society.

From ancient Greece and Rome came a secular humanism also basic to Western (including American) thought. This humanism expressed itself in ideas and attitudes that have lived on into the twentieth century:

1. A speculative philosophy that deals with the nature of man and of the larger reality of which he is a part.
2. The idea that knowledge has a value in itself; that science, based on accurate observation and correct logic, is an instrument for understanding nature; and that history is a means for making man aware of himself and his values.
3. The idea of an order in the universe and in society capable of discovery by human observation and reason.
4. The idea of natural law in human relations embodying the principles of justice that transcend the capricious wills of men and their rulers and justify hope and expectations of progress toward more perfect human societies.
5. The idea of art as disciplined forms reflecting man in his environment and expressing his feelings, his traditions, and his

beliefs. From Greece, the idea of architecture as an expression of proportion and harmony, and from Rome, as an expression of interior space.

The mind of Western civilization, including that of its American variant, has been conditioned by the events and developments that followed the defeat of the Roman Empire by the peoples of Western and Northern Europe. The European followers of the Christian tradition early divided into an Eastern Orthodox church, which had its center at Constantinople, and a Roman Catholic church, which had its center at Rome. In the centuries of confusion and disorder that followed the fall of Rome, a feudal system of interpersonal relationships and mutual obligations arose and maintained a measure of social discipline. On the baron rested the obligation to defend with his armed knights and his fortified castle the freemen and serfs of his domain. Birth fixed the status of the individual person, and an oath bound subordinates to their liege lord.

The hierarchical order of feudalism and the universal authority of the Catholic church and the Holy Roman Empire were shattered by the rise of new nations. Each nation was defended by royal armies using gunpowder, justified by the political philosophy of Machiavelli and Bodin attributing sovereignty to the prince, and came to be unified by vernacular literature made available by the new printing press, making people aware of common language and stimulating loyalty to the nation. The devastating wars of religion led to the peace of Westphalia which assumed an order, universal in principle but at first confined in practice to Europe, of territorial states equal in the fact of their independence, with relations regulated by the law of nature and nations expounded by Francis of Vitoria and Hugo Grotius.

During the several centuries in which feudalism provided the primary system for regulating society, the Roman Catholic church, spreading Christianity over Western and Northern

Europe, existed as a unifying force amid the diversity of peoples and cultures. Churches and monasteries were built from Sicily to Britain and from Spain to the Baltic. The church not only extended its doctrines and its authority in religious matters throughout the area, but its monasteries preserved the writings of the ancient Greek and Roman world. Out of a desire to extend as well as to preserve learning grew the first universities.

For some centuries after the fall of Rome, the Byzantine Empire extended outward from its capital, Constantinople, into Central and Eastern Europe. It carried to its frontiers the Eastern Orthodox church and its own variations of the arts associated with Christian worship and those with secular life. A new era began to dawn for the West as increasingly busy trade routes brought commercial and artistic products from as far away as China and the East Indies to the Mediterranean cities of Venice and Genoa. From these centers of commerce, goods from the East found their way to the towns and castles of Western Europe. As the trade with Asia became important for Europeans in the fifteenth and sixteenth centuries, nation-states already mentioned began emerging from feudalism—in particular, Portugal, Spain, France, and England. The change did not mean that feudalism disappeared, but rather that the monarch became supreme among feudal lords and established his rule within the boundaries of a nation. Contemporaneous with the emergence of nation-states came the discovery of a new world and the opening of an age of exploration and of adventuring by Europeans outside their continent. At the same time occurred a rediscovery of a new emphasis upon the humanism, learning, and art of ancient Greece, leading to naturalism in art and to the development of rational and experimental science.

Amid the intellectual ferment caused by the new perspectives opened by the appearance of the nation-state, the widening geographical horizon, and the emerging of a scientific method, there developed in different parts of Europe revolts against the ecclesiastical authority of the Roman church and against the theological doctrines on which that authority rested. The revolts also sought to end abuses that had arisen within the church. As a consequence of the movements of protest, different Protestant churches made their appearance, especially in the German states, in Scandinavia, in Switzerland, in Holland, and in England.

The expansion of Europe beyond its continental limits stimulated trade. The nation-states assisted and regulated the new trading ventures. An economic system of private enterprise appeared in which interpersonal relationships were governed by contract. Because of its emphasis on the accumulation and management of capital, it was called capitalism. Like the nation-state, capitalism grew up beside feudalism, affecting it but not supplanting it. The variety of Protestantism originated by John Calvin in Switzerland and in seventeenth-century England, called Puritanism, reinforced capitalism by sanctifying work (the creation of capital) and by emphasizing saving through refraining from luxurious or riotous living (the accumulation of capital).

In the sixteenth century, Portugal established settlements in Brazil. At the same time Spain, after conquering advanced American Indian civilizations, built an empire that extended over the remainder of the South American continent and in North America as far as California, Texas, and Florida. In the seventeenth century, different groups of Englishmen, with the approval of the king but not acting under his formal direction, created settlements along the Atlantic coast. Here the scattered tribes of American Indians had not advanced beyond a hunting and gardening stone-age culture. The red men, however, contributed to the Europeans plants they had domesticated; in particular, tobacco and maize. Also in the seventeenth century, France sent pioneers to the valley of the St. Lawrence and to Nova Scotia and, at the beginning of the eighteenth, to the mouth of the Mississippi.

These sixteenth-, seventeenth-, and eighteenth-century immigrants from Europe carried to the New World the Portuguese, Spanish, English, and French variants of Western civilization. The

English variant, first planted on the western shore of the Atlantic from Maine to Georgia, became the United States. But in the course of something more than three centuries, the population of what became the United States took on an ethnic diversification. Large numbers of migrants came, particularly in the nineteenth and early twentieth centuries, from all parts of Europe and in small numbers from Asia. Beginning in the seventeenth century, Europeans brought Negroes from Africa to the New World to supply the need for labor. At the beginning of the nineteenth century, the United States put an end to the importation of slaves. But Africa had contributed an element of considerable size to the population of the nation. Back of the mid-twentieth-century generation of citizens of the United States lies, therefore, an extraordinary ethnic mingling. Ethnic diversity, however, has not prevented the evolution of a unified national culture. The discussions that follow deal with that culture.

American Values in Politics

American values in politics find their source in the political thought of seventeenth-century England. In that century Parliament, after a long evolution that began in feudal times, emerged as a firmly established lawmaking body. In 1688 Parliament achieved supremacy when that body forced the abdication of James II and invited William and Mary to the throne. The event marked the final triumph of the principles that the people, through their elected representatives, should possess ultimate governmental authority.

John Locke, English philosopher, in arguments intended to justify the bloodless "Revolution of 1688," elaborated political theories that in the eighteenth century made a powerful impact on European and colonial American thought. He reaffirmed the old theory of compact; namely, that men, originally to put an end to the anarchy of life in a state of nature, entered into a compact with one another to establish a government. Locke tied to the idea of compact a theory of natural rights. If the Author of Nature created man as a rational and independent being, consistency required that man possess natural rights to life, to liberty, and to property. By property Locke meant the clothing, habitations, and tools that enabled men to maintain life. Locke insisted that when men entered into a compact to establish government, they charged that government with the primary responsibility of defending and preserving these natural rights. If an established government fails in this obligation to preserve the rights to life, liberty, or property, it may lawfully be changed. Locke provided a theoretical foundation for the principle of government by consent of the governed.

The circumstances of the founding in the seventeenth century of English colonies on the mainland of North America helped the transfer of British political institutions and values to the New World. The English government as such founded no colony. The Crown rather gave legal authorization to private companies, to groups of persons, or to single persons on their own initiative to found colonies. In the New World the colonists, after difficult first years of adjustment, found ample natural resources to make possible self-sufficient settlements. The American Indians who lived neighbor to these settlements, although they posed a threat, did not represent a danger of such magnitude as to require rigid discipline on the part of the settlers or the maintenance of military garrisons for defense. The conditions of the first English frontier in North America tended to give importance to the individual colonist. He must chop out a clearing in the forest and establish a farm. He must be prepared, as a militiaman, to defend his settlement against an occasional Indian attack. The task of establishing civilization in the seventeenth-century American wilderness was of vast magnitude, and the men to accomplish it were few. This ratio of few men to land extending endlessly westward from the ocean established the importance of the individual person in the society of the seventeenth-century frontier.

The settlers who came from England to occupy and to extend this frontier considered that they brought with them the rights of Englishmen. Colonial charters, either specifically or by implication, confirmed that the rights possessed in the Motherland would be retained in the colonies. Chief among these rights was that to share in government through elected representatives. Beginning with Virginia in 1619, colonials in all the provinces elected representative assemblies which made local laws and levied local taxes. In each colony the franchise was limited by property qualifications or for religious reasons. In more thickly settled New England, the men of the towns came together periodically in town meetings to decide by the method of direct democracy upon the disposition of the affairs of the town. The conditions of life on the seventeenth-century frontier, therefore, with its large measure of freedom and with its emphasis on the importance of the individual person, provided an auspicious setting for the principle of government by consent of the governed.

In the eighteenth century, the British colonies in North America expanded, increased in population, and prospered in a favorable environment. Germans and Scotch-Irish who immigrated in substantial numbers at this time, when added to the Swedes and Dutch who had come in the seventeenth century, created an ethnic complexity that was to characterize the American population increasingly in the later national period. But the political ideas and patterns derived from England continued to be the norms.

In 1776, after a decade of efforts on the part of the British government to increase and strengthen imperial control, the colonies on the mainland of North America revolted and declared their independence. The rebellion against imperial authority began, however, as a fight for the ''rights of Englishmen,'' threatened by a succession of measures that tended to reduce the authority of the colonial assemblies by enabling the imperial government to tax colonials or to take other measures to assert directly the authority of the king over his American subjects. The

American Declaration of Independence, written by Thomas Jefferson and adopted by the Continental Congress, affirmed that the primary reason for the action was the attempt on the part of the imperial government to make free men in the colonies subject to external power in the direction of which they had no share. The Declaration made the classic statement of the doctrine of political liberty as held by eighteenth-century Americans and by their successors to the present. It follows:

> We hold these truths to be self-evident, that all men are created equal, that they are endowed by their Creator with certain unalienable Rights, that among these are Life, Liberty and the Pursuit of Happiness—that to secure these rights, Governments are instituted among Men, deriving their just powers from the consent of the governed. That whenever any Form of Government becomes destructive of these ends, it is the Right of the people to alter or to abolish it, and to institute new Government. . . .

During the Revolutionary War most of the newly independent states substituted written constitutions for the old colonial charters. The constitution of Massachusetts contained the specific affirmation that it was a compact. It also included a bill of rights which, spelling out natural rights in detail, gave them legal status as civil rights. In 1781 Americans established a Confederation to which the states ceded claims to western lands to be governed by the Congress until carved into new states. George Washington, commander-in-chief of the armies of the rebellion, led the Revolution to its successful conclusion in 1783, nearly eight years after he accepted his commission. When peace came, Washington, in an action intended to confirm the supremacy of civil over military authority, appeared before the Continental Congress and surrendered his commission to its president.

In 1787, four years after the close of the Revolutionary War, representatives of the states meeting in convention at Philadelphia drafted a written constitution for the United States that, superseding the Confederation, established the nation as a Federal Republic. The ratification of this Constitution by the states made it the supreme law of the land. The people of the United States, through their representatives in the Constitutional Convention and in the ratifying conventions of the states, had of their own will established their own government. Almost immediately after the inauguration of the new government, a Bill of Rights was added to the Constitution. These first amendments enumerated the necessary rights of free men in a self-governing nation and gave them the legal status of civil rights.

Out of the heritage from England, the experience with government in the colonies, the struggle for independence, the weakness of the Confederation, the creation of the Federal Republic, and the experience of more than a century and a half of independence, including four years of civil war (1861-1865), have come American values in the area of politics:

1. The concept of the state as a utilitarian device created to provide for the common defense and to further the general welfare.

2. Freedom and responsibility of the individual adult citizen to have a voice in the government under which he lives, as exemplified in the right and responsibility to vote.

3. Freedom of access to knowledge of all kinds save only when disclosure of particular information would endanger the whole community. This access is achieved through a system of public education, the practice of academic freedom, and the existence of a free press.

4. Freedom to express orally or in writing opinions honestly held concerning economic, religious, political, or social matters. In the case of political opinions, this freedom is limited by the requirements that actions to carry opinions into effect must conform to the procedures for changing the policies or structure of the

state as set forth in the Constitution of the United States. A further general limitation is that expression of opinion must not be so inciting as to create a clear and present danger of panic or disorder.

5. The protection of the free citizen against unreasonable invasions of privacy by officers of government.

6. The right of free citizens to assemble peaceably.

7. The supremacy of civil authority over the military in conformity with the principle that the civil authority is the decision-making power and the military is the instrument, when needed, to carry decisions into effect.

8. The concept of the American Federation as a "permanent union of permanent states," firmly established after the Civil War, maintained by judicial enforcement of the Constitution and forbidding nullification or secession on the part of the states.

Efforts throughout our national history to realize fully the principle of citizen participation in government suggest the evolutionary character of American values. By the end of the first third of the nineteenth century, practically all of the states had extended the right to vote to all male citizens twenty-one or over. As the century ended, most of the states had passed laws requiring that a voter cast his ballot in secret. These laws were intended to prevent the improper manipulation of elections by threats or bribery of electors. In 1920 an amendment to the Constitution gave to women citizens the right to vote. In the first half of the twentieth century, the states in the southern part of the United States, where Negroes were very numerous, sharply limited by legislative enactment or by administrative procedures the number of Negro citizens permitted to vote. In the middle decades of the century, the Supreme Court of the United States struck down these enactments and administrative procedures that came within its jurisdiction on the ground that they were contrary to the Constitution, which by amendment after the Civil War forbade any limitation of voting on grounds of "race, color, or previous condition of servitude." In

1960 Congress enacted a second measure which gave to the federal courts specific powers to insure the right to vote to any citizen illegally deprived of it. Accelerating urbanization in the twentieth century caused in several states an inequality of representation in legislatures between citizens dwelling in cities and those of rural areas. When rural districts refused to surrender their improper advantage, the Supreme Court found unequal representation a violation of the Constitution and required offending states to redistrict.

American experience has proven that even constitutional government does not nullify the validity of the ancient adage that power tends to corrupt. In the fierce competition for public office, candidates have occasionally been guilty of venality or have practiced fraud. Also, elected and appointed officials have sometimes used the powers of public office for private gain. To correct abuses in political campaigns, Congress has enacted legislation regulating contributions to political parties and dealing with their expenditures in such contests. Through appropriate committees Congress has investigated officials and agencies charged with administrative responsibilities. It has turned its attention to the formulation of rules of behavior for the guidance of public officials. The misdeeds of a small minority have emphasized, however, that for the majority public office is a public trust.

Since the establishment of the nation, each generation of Americans has faced in one form or another the problem of maintaining freedom of speech and of the press. The exercise of these rights has at one time or another been threatened in local communities where tensions arising out of religious, racial, or political issues exacerbated the relations between a dominant majority and a dissenting minority. In the decade following the close of World War II, some public anxiety concerning the extent of subversive activities within the nation raised the problem again. The conviction on grounds of conspiracy of the leaders of the American Communist party added to tensions created by the discovery that certain government employees had passed classified information to a foreign power. These and later political developments of a related nature precipitated a series of widespread official investigations in public spheres, in private industry working under government contract, and among private institutions and organizations. This in turn led to a series of highly publicized accusations and counter accusations and public hearings which were covered by press, radio, and television and given national and to some extent international publicity. This episode, occurring just after the turn of mid-twentieth century, is one that is so well known at home and abroad that it needs no further elaboration. Among the results of this dramatic period, there emerged a general strengthening of public appreciation of the importance of the basic freedoms and the necessity for constant vigilance to protect those freedoms.

Law in American Values

The evolution of Western civilization brought forth two distinct legal systems. For much of Western Europe, modern law springs from that law which was the supreme expression of the genius of the ancient Romans. Roman law was clear, precise, and could be expressed in code. From it as a source came French and German law. Although England was for three centuries part of the Roman Empire, Roman law did not make a permanent impress on this province of the northern frontier.

After the fall of Rome and at the height of the feudal system, the English common law came into being. The English law courts attempted to apply the principles of justice in disputes or in criminal actions before them. In general, they found justice best served in civil litigations by deciding according to the time-honored custom of the localities. In such litigations the English courts of feudal times called in a jury of men from the localities to determine, after hearing the evidence presented, the facts in the dispute. The judge interpreted the law. In criminal cases the defendant had the right to have the truth or falsity of the charges against him determined by a jury of his peers. English common law came into being in the feudal centuries when the evolution of the English Parliament was beginning. The two were alike in one particular. Through Parliament the commoner shared in government; through the jury system he shared in the administration of justice.

The common law courts of England set forth their decisions. Courts, when deciding cases, studied and applied precedents established by the decision of judges in similar actions of earlier date. The corpus of court decisions, growing through the centuries, constituted the essence of the common law. The common law evolved as society evolved and customs changed. But it changed on a fixed base, because the ultimate objective of law was to do justice and the principles of justice were deemed to be eternal. The common law was not made wholly by the courts. Occasional far-reaching acts of the evolving Parliament dealing with human relations and human rights became part of the corpus.

Out of this evolution of legal principles and practices came in England the concept of law as an entity over against the king, who in the feudal period was not much more than chief among the barons. At his coronation the king pledged to obey the law and to deal justly with his subjects. In this expressed contract between the monarch and his subjects may be found the seeds of the later concept of "a government of law and not of men."

Englishmen inevitably brought the outlook and practices of the common law to the New World. In the first half of the nineteenth century, after a profession of trained lawyers had come into being and after learned American lawyers had written legal treatises, the common law fitted well the conditions of life in colonial and national America. From the beginnings of settlement, change was a fundamental characteristic of American life. In the seventeenth century, the struggling colonies achieved stability. In the eighteenth century, Americans made good their independence and created a Federal Republic. They pushed their settlement westward across North America and established civilization in an area as large as Europe. In this same century they transformed a predominantly agricultural civilization into a highly developed industrial civilization. The principles of flexibility and adaptability in the common law made it peculiarly applicable to American conditions. It evolved in America in ways appropriate to American life. In the words of Justice Oliver Wendell Holmes of the Supreme Court of the United States, law springs out of "experience." Out of experience has come, in particular, the safeguards in American law designed to protect the free man against tyranny on the part of the constituted authority. Evolving American values in the field of law include the following concepts:

1. The concept of a "government of law and not of men." In the United States this means the supremacy of law administered by the regular courts over the officers and agencies of government.

2. The concept of law as a living growth, changing with the evolution of society.

3. The right of every person to be free to move about and to choose his occupation, unless convicted of crime and subject only to the general law, thus forbidding slavery or involuntary servitude.

4. The right of every person to be informed specifically of any charges made by the state against him, to speedy and public trial, to compulsory process for obtaining witnesses, and to legal counsel assuring him equal protection of the laws.

5. The right of a person to refuse to testify against himself. This right prevents the forced and often false confession that is a most revolting aspect of totalitarian tyranny.

6. The right to a trial by a jury of peers when the United States government brings the charges. In some states a defendant has the option to choose trial by a judge.

7. The protection of persons from being "twice put in jeopardy of life or limb" for the same offense or, if convicted, from "cruel or unusual punishments."

8. The denial to government of the power to punish a person through the instrumentality of an *ex post facto* law, that is, a law formulated to make an act an offense after the act has taken place.

The problem of maintaining social order, common to every society, has been complicated in the United States by certain peculiarities in the development of the nation. In the late eighteenth and in the nineteenth centuries, the American people spread their settlements westward into a virtually empty wilderness until they reached the Pacific Ocean. Sparse population and rudimentary arrangements for maintaining order characterized the westward-moving margin of settlement. Frontier communities put a high premium on individual initiative and self-reliance. The frontier situation also gave unusual opportunities for lawlessness. In the early phases of the development of settled society before civil authority had been firmly established, pioneers often organized extralegal vigilante groups to combat crime and to deal out a rough justice. The frontier emphasis on individual initiative and self-reliance persisted as a fundamental American attitude. The tendency toward lawlessness continued in a small proportion of the population and on occasion found expression in mob violence and racial discrimination. Lawlessness later found expression in the giant cities created by nineteenth- and twentieth-century industrialism in the gangsterism of the underworld. This gangsterism existed in urban societies characterized by a diversity of ethnic elements. The flood of immigration of the nineteenth and early twentieth centuries poured men and women from a great variety of countries into American cities. Ethnic and racial diversity also, on occasion, stimulated violence against newer immigrants or persons of other races on the part of lower class citizens born of older American stocks.

The perennial problem of maintaining social order has given a special importance in American thought and practice to the value described in the phrase "a government of law and not of men." This value has found legal expression in the written constitutions of the fifty states of the Republic and in that of the United States. In the American federal system, ordinary police power rests with the states and with the municipalities created by the states. State and local police deal with crimes of violence and fraud, enforce laws regulating the family, and administer motor vehicle and traffic regulations. The police power of the federal government operates in the area of the enforcement of treaties, of the federal laws, and of the orders of federal courts.

The chief institutional expression of the value of a "government of law" is the court of justice. The constitution of each of the fifty states and that of the United States affirms the principle of the independence of the judiciary. The judge, in presiding at the bench or in formulating his decisions in his chambers, maintains a complete independence of the executive and the legislative branches of government. This independence stems from the wider principle of "checks and balances" in American government. Under the Constitution of the United States and of the states, all three branches—executive, legislative, and judicial—operate independently, and each has definite checks upon the others. The Supreme Court on many occasions has invalidated laws enacted by Congress on the ground that they contravened the "supreme law of the land"; namely, the Constitution of the United States. At the same time, the Supreme Court through more than a century and a half has interpreted the "supreme law" in a flexible manner with the result that a constitution written for an eighteenth-century agrarian society meets adequately the needs of a mid-twentieth-century industrial civilization. In the states the police systems and the courts have maintained order within a society in which the appearance of the giant metropolis has added to the complexities of ethnic diversity.

The great city in the United States spawned the problem of the delinquent juvenile, though the phenomenon is not limited to large urban centers. Both government and the more thoughtful among the population are alerted to the situation. Social scientists have explored the causes of the phenomenon and have suggested useful ways of dealing with the younger generation. American society has created a great variety of nongovernmental character-building agencies and institutions, such as the Boy Scouts, to guide youth along the difficult road to adulthood. The police and juvenile courts have played a constructive role. But the problem of delinquency of youth, as of adults, is perennial.

In 1954 an epoch-making decision of the Supreme Court reflected a growing public concern for civil rights. The Court declared that segregation of races in tax-supported school systems is contrary to that provision of the Constitution which guarantees to all citizens the "equal protection of the laws." Racial segregation in schools had from the time of the Civil War been the custom in those southern states where slavery persisted until that conflict and where the percentage of Negroes in the population was high. The process of desegregation proceeded slowly after the decision, occurring most readily in those communities of the South that lay nearer to its northern border. The episode suggests the power and importance of the courts in the American governmental system.

In the middle decades of the twentieth century, Americans expanded the role of law. Referring only to the federal government, they used law as an instrument for the regulation of the economy—manufacturing, commerce and agriculture, management and labor. They used law for purposes of social engineering—the establishment of the services and the creation of the agencies to further the general welfare—social security arrangements, the Tennessee Valley Authority (an agency for the development of a geographically definable area). The law under which the people live has become a complex of legislative enactments, rules of administrative agencies, and judicial interpretations. It has its confusions and its uncertainties. But, in spite of these, it has through the years ordered the behavior alike of private citizens and public officials.

Religion in American Values

The religious aspect of the culture of the United States expresses the Judeo-Christian tradition central to Western civilization. The faith of the great majority of the men and women of the seventeenth and eighteenth centuries who laid the foundations of American civilization was that of one or another of the varieties of Protestantism. In several colonies the Church of England was, after the pattern of the Mother Country, the established church. In England in the first half of the seventeenth century, Puritans, influenced by the teachings of John Calvin of Geneva, tried to modify the forms of worship of the Anglican church. The tension and the persecution which resulted caused many thousands of them to migrate to the New World where they founded colonies in which the churches taught the Puritan doctrine and worshipped after the plain Puritan manner. More radical Protestant sects founded still other colonies. These sects, particularly the Baptists and the Society of Friends, challenged the normal pattern of the age by demanding the separation of church and state and freedom of worship for all men. In addition to the Protestant refugees from persecution at the hands of the rulers of England, a small company of Roman Catholic refugees founded a colony. In the eighteenth century, German migrants brought sects, such as that of the Moravians, to the English colonies. The history of Christianity in what became the United States began, therefore, in diversity.

After the confirmation of independence with the successful outcome of the Revolutionary War, Virginia disestablished the former Anglican, now Episcopalian, church and granted religious freedom to all citizens. In the last decade of the eighteenth century, the First Amendment to the Constitution of the United States forbade the federal government to make any religious establishment and extended religious liberty throughout the nation.

In the nineteenth and early twentieth centuries, millions of immigrants, mostly from Europe, came to the United States. Large numbers of these belonged to the Roman Catholic faith. As a result, that church became the largest single denomination in the United States. Other immigrants brought Judaism, the Eastern Orthodox church, and other varieties of Protestantism. Immigrants coming from Asia in small numbers brought Islam, Buddhism, Hinduism, and Sikhism. In these same nineteenth and twentieth centuries, Americans originated new Protestant denominations and created three variants of Christianity that have spread beyond the boundaries of the nation. These are the Church of Christ of the Latter Day Saints (Mormon), Christian Science, and the Watch Tower Society (Jehovah's Witnesses). In the mid-twentieth century, a time marked by great interest in religion among the citizens of the Republic, a strong ecumenical movement brought an increasing measure of unity in American Protestantism. At the same time the three major faiths—Protestantism, Roman Catholicism, and Judaism—have increasingly practiced cooperation in the areas of relief and welfare.

Side by side with religion has gone a secular humanism that stems ultimately from classical Greece. It appeared in the English colonies in the middle of the eighteenth century in the form of the Enlightenment whose center was France. This humanism emphasizing reason and science achieved a major importance in American thought in the decades immediately following the American Revolution. It suffered a decline at the turn of the nineteenth century, partly as a result of the horror of Americans at the excesses of the French Revolution, which many citizens of the United States attributed to the new rationalism.

In the nineteenth century, the tradition of humanistic rationalism continued as Unitarianism and the liberalization of some orthodox denominations. In the twentieth century, supported by the triumphs of science, humanistic rationalism became for a second time important in American thought.

From this experience of religious faith through more than three centuries and from the experience of faith in humanistic rationalism for more than two have come the values of religion in American life. They include the following concepts and goals:

1. The idea that the state is not coterminous with society but that religious institutions exist of their own right in society independent of the state—the separation of church and state.

2. The freedom to believe and to propagate one's faith as the conscience of the individual person directs, or freedom to refrain from worship. This freedom of worship does not extend to practices that debase the community.

3. The idea of the church as a free association of believers who assume responsibility for its support.

4. The widespread but not universal emphasis on some form of theism as a frame for explaining the meaning of human life.

5. The idea, widely but not universally held, that ethical standards spring from religion.

6. The idea that the furthering of the brotherhood of man under the fatherhood of God calls for the outreach of the churches to the far corners of the world on errands of mercy, to assist social evolution toward a better life, and to further mutually helpful cooperation among all peoples.

7. A sense of charity, stemming in part from the humanistic tradition and in part from that of Judeo-Christianity, coupled with the idea that the performance of acts that contribute to the well-being of individual persons and of society are in themselves religious activities of merit. Some of the religious beliefs and practices are closer to the understandings and teachings of social psychology than they are to traditional spiritual doctrines. Historically, religion in America has created educational and humanitarian institutions, and the practice continues.

8. The idea that the state must respect the convictions of the conscientious objector to refrain from participation in the bloody violence of war, but that the state may require of the conscientious objector in time of emergency special service of a nonviolent nature.

American churches, being human institutions, have often through the centuries reflected the thought of the time and place in which they existed. In the middle of the nineteenth century, when the issues of slavery and the preservation of the Union divided the nation to the point of bringing on a civil war, several of the great Protestant denominations divided into northern organizations that opposed slavery and southern branches that supported the customs and institutions of that section. In the twentieth century, most of these divisions have been healed, but custom continued the separate Negro and white churches that had appeared after the abolition of slavery. In the middle of the twentieth century, however, many churches both Protestant and Catholic have opposed segregation of the races and have encouraged membership from among both racial groups.

In the early nineteenth century, when American churches first sought to reach out to the non-Christian world, their representatives abroad tended to emphasize almost exclusively the message of faith. In the twentieth century, these churches, responding to the needs of peoples in other lands, sent out medical, educational, and agricultural aid, while at the same time they sought to assist the growth of indigenous churches.

In the nineteenth century, the religious pattern of the United States emerged as three primary but unequal divisions—the Protestant majority, a Roman Catholic minority stemming mainly from nineteenth- and twentieth-century migrants, and the small Jewish minority constituting an important element in New York and other large cities. Because of the wide differences existing between these three groups, religious teaching and the practices of worship were reduced to a minimum in all tax-supported elementary and secondary schools. This secularization of the state schools brought about the development of independent, privately supported schools by some Protestant denominations and by the Roman Catholics. At the same time emphasis on religious instruction of the young within houses of worship became a major activity of the three principal religious groups.

A great popular interest in religion characterized the middle years of the twentieth century. A British observer, Barbara Ward, remarked in her "Report to Europe on America," "The fact of a religious revival in America cannot be gainsaid." Membership in synagogues and churches increased at a greater rate than did the population. Attendance upon places of worship, sales of books of religious interest, and nationwide audiences of particular religious programs on radio and television, when taken together, evidenced an attention to religion surpassing that of any previous period in our history when the entire population is considered. This visible movement of the times acted as a stimulus to the creation of religious music and to the improvement of its rendition. New houses of worship to meet the needs of a growing membership sometimes held fast to the traditional Gothic style of the Middle Ages or the classical style of the Renaissance. With increasing frequency, however, the new sanctuaries sought to express religious aspiration through new architectural forms and new variations of old symbols. This manifestation of religious interest occurred in an age of tension and anxiety when the threat of nuclear warfare hung over the world and when abroad a frankly materialistic religion, denying all gods, challenged Judeo-Christianity.

Education in American Values

In the seventeenth and eighteenth centuries, English colonials on the continent of North America placed on parents the responsibility for the education of their children. Local schools for training in reading and writing appeared, particularly in New England. Many families hired private tutors. Latin schools to prepare students for entrance upon work in higher education came into being in the larger towns. In these centuries institutions of higher learning grew up, usually initiated by religious leaders and normally receiving some support from the state. These institutions imitated the form of the colleges of Oxford and Cambridge and in the beginning were known as colleges.

As the nation expanded westward to the Pacific in the first half of the nineteenth century, the basic national law which governed the process of evolution of frontier communities into sovereign states provided for the establishment of elementary schools. Almost at the beginning of our national history, the Tenth Amendment to the Constitution reserved to the states powers which the Constitution had not specifically granted to the federal government. Among these powers retained by the state was the control of education. From this basic decision has grown the practice of decentralization of responsibility for education. The activities of the federal government in the field of education are sharply circumscribed. During the first half of the nineteenth century in the older eastern states, private secondary schools called academies increased. In these states and in the younger communities of the interior of the continent, colleges, founded for the most part by churches, proliferated. These institutions, some strong and some weak, came to be scattered over most of the nation. Normally, their curricula emphasized the liberal arts.

In the second quarter of the nineteenth century, individual states began to establish elementary schools supported by taxation and at the same time normal schools for training teachers. These two developments marked the beginning of a system of public schools that in time became universal throughout the nation. In the second half of the century, most of the states enacted laws requiring attendance at school usually to the age of sixteen, with permission to leave for reason of work at age fourteen. By the turn of the twentieth century, the tax-supported secondary school, the high school, had become established and over the nation had supplanted in significance the earlier independent academy. In the first half of the twentieth century, the tax-supported high school became universal throughout the United States. In the middle of that century, approximately 75 percent of the sixteen- and seventeen-year-old Americans were enrolled in full-time education in these schools.

In 1862 Congress passed the Morrill Act allocating to the several states economic aid to enable them to establish colleges of "agriculture and the mechanic arts." The state universities that rose out of this action became in the twentieth century the most characteristic American institutions of higher learning. From the beginning, the principle prevailed in them that training youth for later life activities is a proper function of formal higher education. In these universities, schools of agriculture and engineering, pharmacy, dentistry, medicine, law, and many other specialized vocations came into being to provide systematic instruction. From the beginning, also, the state universities included instruction in the liberal arts. In the mid-twentieth century, they provide at the same time specialized and general education. Many of these state universities have grown to great size. Some have student bodies of 20,000 or more. At the same time the state universities were developing, some of the liberal arts colleges dating from the colonial period or from the nineteenth century, independent of tax support and based on private endowments, evolved into universities whose scholarship gave them a rank equal to any in the world. In 1958 the percentage of eighteen- and nineteen-year-olds attending institutions of higher learning was 37.6. The percentage is constantly increasing.

In the course of this evolution of the school system of the nation, American values in education have emerged. They include the following concepts:

1. The idea that effective self-government requires that a significant proportion of the electorate have sufficient education to be able to inform themselves of issues and to consider them rationally.

2. The idea that equality of educational opportunity for all citizens is the just and desirable foundation for a democratic society.

3. The idea that the state has an obligation not only to provide educational opportunities from kindergarten through the university, but to require children to attend school until their early teens.

4. The idea that the state should not have a monopoly of education and that independent, privately supported schools, colleges, and universities bring to the educational system a diversity and variety that further the general welfare.

5. The idea that education, particularly advanced education, by training specialists to work in a society which emphasizes specialization, increases the opportunities of the individual person to find for himself a useful place in the community and to achieve an income commensurate with his abilities.

6. The idea that from the elementary grades to the bachelor's degree, the school exists for the training of the student as a social being as well as for the cultural enrichment of the individual and the training of the mind.

7. At the level of the university, the idea that general education should precede or pace side by side with the training of the specialist to the end that the specially trained person have breadth of view and flexibility of mind along with a particular competence.

8. The idea of academic freedom which asserts that teachers in higher education should be free to search for and to teach the truth as they see it without compulsion from the state, the church, the business community, or the administrative authorities of the institution and to this end should enjoy security of tenure.

9. The idea that education should be a lifelong process and that

opportunities for postschool training should be available to adults, as far as practicable.

In such a gigantic educational undertaking as that of the United States, gaps appeared between ideals and their realization. In the middle of the twentieth century, important problems connected with mass education at the elementary and secondary levels appeared. The school systems of the states encountered difficulty in finding a sufficient number of qualified teachers to meet the needs of a rapidly growing school population. The tendency was noted for schools attempting to cope with large enrollments to direct their primary attention to the great middle group of mediocre students, to the disadvantage of the gifted pupil. In the middle years of the twentieth century, school officials and an interested public were aware of these problems, and vigorous efforts were underway to improve both situations.

In the twentieth century, universities initiated and supported by cities or other local communities appeared beside the older state universities to meet the needs of a growing youth population that desired training beyond the high school level. Inevitably, there were marked differences in standards among the great number of institutions, tax-supported and independent, that offered higher education. To meet this problem, colleges and universities united to create an organization for the purpose of watching standards. This organization exercises the disciplinary power of refusing to accredit colleges or universities found to be substandard. Such refusal of accreditation means that undergraduates in institutions publicly marked as inferior suffer grave disadvantage when they wish to transfer to other institutions or to enter postgraduate professional schools. This device for self-discipline among institutions of higher learning has acted to maintain proper standards. But public criticism and withdrawal of confidence has been the primary sanction for the enforcement of quality.

As the twentieth century advanced, educational opportunity

increased for Americans. The number of awards and scholarships available, along with part-time jobs to help meet university expenses, have put higher education within the reach of practically every young man or woman who desires it and who has the capacity to profit by it. To meet the needs of adult education, universities, both tax-supported and independent, have developed extension services to carry the learning accumulated by research to the ordinary citizen. The extension service reaches into farm communities to assist the agriculturist, into nonspecialized communities to provide information needed for intelligent discussion of public issues, and into homes to give aid to the housewife in the rearing of her family and in the performance of her household tasks. The increasing use of television for some of these services has helped to close the gap between public demand and the ability of the extension services of the universities to respond.

The desire of people, both adults and children, for education and intellectual recreation outside the formal educational program led in the nineteenth century to the development of free libraries, open to the public. The support of community libraries is now generally recognized as the responsibility of local government with assistance from state and federal government in extending and improving service. The typical public library in the United States not only lends books, but conducts an active program to encourage reading and studying. The art museums, which exist in every important city, also make available to the public as part of their normal activities not only special exhibitions but art lectures. They also periodically present shows of the best work in the fine arts done by artists in their locality. The less common museums of natural history, where they exist, organize the display of their materials for the purpose of furthering public education. The National Parks Service of the United States supervises the many scenic and historical national parks scattered throughout the country. In most of the parks, trained naturalists or historians give lectures to the public or lead parties of visitors on trips for the purpose of providing better understanding of the natural features or the historical significance of the parks. The impact of this form of adult education is suggested by the fact that millions of visitors come each year to the national parks.

Social Values

Historically, American social values spring from the religious and humanistic strands in Western civilization. But the conditions of life in the New World from the very beginning of the English settlement have shaped the American outlook and given a particular stamp to American social values. The condition of primary importance lies in the fact that English settlers coming to the colonies on the mainland brought the institution of feudalism with them only in shadowy form. Lord Baltimore, proprietor and colonizer of Maryland, had a quasi-feudal relationship to the settlers in the area. The Dutch founded semi-feudal landed estates along the banks of the Hudson River. There were other but unimportant suggestions of feudalism in colonial arrangements. The Englishmen and other Europeans who came to the English colonies accepted class distinctions as normal to society. But the British nobility, with rare exceptions, did not come to America. The feudal aristocracy of Europe had no counterpart in the English colonies of the seventeenth and eighteenth centuries. The Puritan leaders who founded colonies in New England were by European standards members of the middle class. The statement holds in general for the leading colonials in all other English colonies. Many of the settlers were laborers. Some, too poor to pay their passage, sold their labor in America as indentured servants for a period of years. Some prisoners from British jails were sent to the New World, most of them as indentured servants. From the beginning, social distinctions characterized the life of the colonies. As late as the American Revolution, undergraduates were arranged in the classes of Harvard College and Yale College according to their social position, yet titles rarely appeared. A hereditary aristocracy such as that in France or Britain did not exist.

Beginning in the seventeenth century, Englishmen introduced Negro slavery into their colonies on the mainland and on the sugar-producing islands of the West Indies. Slavery provided a solution to the pressing problem of labor and had its greatest importance on plantations raising staple crops. The slave lost contact with the African culture from which he came. His situation permitted him to acquire only a limited number of the culture traits of his new environment. The consequent inferiority of cultural equipment plus the fact of slavery gave to the Negro a caste status that excluded him from the opportunities of the American open-class system.

The Puritans who settled in New England brought to the New World a code of ethics destined to be of great importance in the development of American values. The Quakers, who founded Pennsylvania near the end of the seventeenth century and who spread widely up and down the Atlantic coast, reinforced the Puritan ethic by teaching a code that was essentially the same. The Puritans glorified work. Their preachers declared that a man worships God by diligent attention to his vocation as well as by attendance upon services of prayer and preaching. The Quakers joined the Puritans in insisting upon that honesty which makes it possible for men of affairs to put confidence in contracts. Both groups taught and practiced the self-denial involved in frugal living which is the foundation of thrift. For both groups a person found his guide in conscience. Benjamin Franklin, who was born in Puritan Boston in the eighteenth century but who made his home in Quaker Philadelphia, removed from the Puritan ethic its theological connotations and turned it into a secular success philosophy—let the individual practice the Puritan virtues, and he can become a man of substance. Franklin gained the attention of thousands of eighteenth-century colonials through his popular publication *Poor Richard's Almanac*, in which his maxims for success appeared. In the first half of the nineteenth century, the two largest denominations of evangelical Protestantism, the Methodists and the Baptists, helped spread the Puritan ethic, again clothed with religious implications, throughout the continental interior and into those South Atlantic states in which in the seventeenth century the Church of England had been the established religion.

Three factors in the American scene, in addition to the ethical code just considered, gave to life in the English colonies its own peculiar development. The failure to transplant feudalism meant the absence in America of a closed-class system. The relative fewness of the settlers compared with the work incident to establishing civilization in a wilderness tended to magnify the importance of the individual person. The freedom and the economic opportunities of the frontier, together with the absence of the limiting taboos of a closed-class system, made it possible for the man of ability and energy to accumulate property and to achieve a position of leadership. The man of humble origins could rise to the top in colonial society. In the eighteenth century, the career of Benjamin Franklin, who began life as a printer's apprentice and rose to international fame, is an extreme example of a progress that was a common phenomenon in all colonies. In the colonies an open-class system appeared in which status was not fixed by birth but was to a great extent determined by individual quality and achievement. This open-class system in the New World together with rich natural resources and a relatively small population made the English colonies and later the United States a land of opportunity. The Declaration of Independence took account of this fundamental characteristic of American life by including among "unalienable rights" that to "the pursuit of happiness."

Many of the men who signed the Declaration recognized the inconsistency between that pronouncement and the fact of Negro slavery. The more northern among the states abolished the institution. It persisted, however, in the warmer portion of the nation where plantation economy was important and where the greatest concentration of Negroes existed. In the middle decades of the nineteenth century, an increasing number of men and women in the North demanded that slavery, with its denial of the "unalienable rights" to "liberty and the pursuit of happiness," be terminated. In the 1860s a prolonged, bloody, and destructive war between the North and the South ended the institution. On January 1, 1863, President Abraham Lincoln by proclamation struck the shackles from the slaves. As free men and women, the Negroes after 1865 took up the long task of learning to share fully in the aspects of American civilization from which they had been excluded.

In the mid-twentieth century, citizens of the United States moved to ameliorate and, if possible, to solve problems associated with two minority groups that had in effect existed since the beginning of the nation. The first of these had to do with the American Indian. The best estimates by anthropologists place the pre-Columbian population of what is now the United States at very roughly 700,000. This population was organized in scores of tribes manifesting wide variations in culture and speaking many different languages. In the seventeenth and eighteenth centuries, the Indians contributed many domestic plants, such as corn and tobacco, to the English settlers along the Atlantic seaboard. The white men also borrowed from their forest neighbors artifacts, among which the canoe was the most important. In those centuries both wars and friendships characterized the relations between the races. In the nineteenth century, the hunting culture of the Indians disappeared as the agricultural civilization of the Americans advanced westward across the continent to the Pacific.

At the end of the nineteenth century, practically all American Indians lived on reservations managed by the federal government. The American Indians were wards of the government, which managed the lands they retained and in some cases paid to the tribes annuities as agreed compensation for tribal land sold to the

United States. In the twentieth century, the federal government provided the tribesmen with schools and a more adequate medical service. As a consequence, the long-continued decline in the population of the American Indians stopped, and they began to increase in numbers. By midcentury the total population included in this minority group was approaching the number estimated for pre-Columbian days. The mid-twentieth-century Indians show great variations in their adjustments to the civilization about them. Such a situation is inevitable because these people do not belong to a homogeneous group. The present-day Indians are descendants of pre-Columbian ancestors who belonged to many different tribes, speaking many different languages and varying from the very primitive culture of the peoples who lived in what is now New England to the high cultural development of the Pueblos of the Southwest. Today in the state of Oklahoma, to which region many of the eastern tribes have moved, many of the Indians have become fully merged into the life of the state. The same is true for some of the Indians resident in New York state. In Oklahoma, moreover, and also in certain areas of the Southwest, a few tribes are very rich because oil or uranium has been discovered on the lands held in trust for them by the United States. There are other tribes located in less desirable areas in the western states who are very poor and who live in part on annuities from the government. The children of some tribes attend the regular public schools near them. Schools maintained by churches or by the United States government serve other tribes. The overall picture shows the American Indians, with variations among the tribes, taking on the traits of the civilization about them, although holding fast to their tribal groups and cherishing tribal traditions at the same time. The government has declared its policy to assist and to encourage the American Indians as individuals to possess as rapidly as possible all the rights and privileges, the freedoms, and responsibilities of other citizens of the nation.

The second problem had to do with the Negro. The relation

between the white and Negro races remains one of the difficult social questions confronting the nation. Its difficulty was appreciably lessened, however, by the fact that a large proportion of the Negro minority had progressed after the Emancipation Proclamation in 1863 to a point in the mid-twentieth century where they were capable of entering fully into the civilization of the nation. The opportunities offered by life in the United States made it possible for a significant number of Negroes to achieve distinction in the professions, in literature, in the arts, and in sports. A Negro scientist living and working in Alabama (in the "Deep South") won an international reputation for his achievements. He was only one of several American Negroes whose fame went round the world. At the same time Negroes in some areas are still poor and need assistance in becoming integrated into the community. After World War II the Supreme Court of the United States, reflecting the temper of a large majority of the citizens of the Republic, handed down a series of decisions designed to give practical effect to the principle embedded in the Constitution that all citizens, without respect to race or color, shall have equal protection of the laws and shall enjoy equal rights in public transport, in voting, and in admission to educational institutions. In 1957 and in 1960, Congress enacted laws the purpose of which is to prevent discrimination on account of race or color against any citizen legally entitled to vote. After the middle of the century in the vast majority of the fifty states in the Union, the integration of Negroes into the political, educational, and economic life of the nation went on steadily and quietly. In a few states bordering on or near the Gulf of Mexico where the percentage of Negroes in the population is high, the principle of integration met opposition on the part of dominant elements in the white population. To meet this opposition and to publicize the cause of equality, Negroes, together with white supporters, staged peaceful demonstrations. The demonstrations themselves provided evidence that old cultural patterns were changing and that in the Deep South also the Negro group was beginning to play a more active role in community life. As Americans pushed further into the second half of the twentieth century, they moved forward on many fronts to give reality to those human rights proclaimed in the Declaration of Independence and confirmed by the Constitution.

In 1959 the United States admitted Hawaii to the Union of sovereign states, with power and status equal to those of the oldest members. This deliberate and considered action gave evidence of dominant American attitudes in the mid-twentieth century. Its significance lay in the fact that in the new state the white population comprises a minority. The majority of the Hawaiian people are of Japanese, Chinese, Philippine, and Polynesian descent. In their first election the citizens of the new state made clear that no racial problem exists in their islands. They chose as one of their senators a man of Chinese descent, as their representative in the House of Representatives, a man of Japanese descent, and as lieutenant governor, a man whose ancestry ran back to the Polynesian Hawaiians who were the original inhabitants of this mid-Pacific archipelago.

Changes have occurred also in other aspects of American society that have brought about modifications in social values. Benjamin Franklin's success philosophy grew out of an agricultural and commercial civilization in which the independent farmer and merchant were leading figures. In such a society both the Puritan code and Franklin's secularized version of it emphasized the isolated individual enterpriser or, in the case of the farmer, the isolated and nearly self-sufficient farm family. In the mid-twentieth century, the individual person finds himself in a world of big business, big labor, big government, even big education. He deals with and is part of bureaucracy, whether of government or of private undertakings. These changed circumstances have brought new emphases to modify the older individualism. Sociability and the capacity to get on with other people have become important for the person who is a member of any one of the great bureaucracies. Impersonal forces move through our industrialized economy. As a consequence, the individual person may suffer damage or even disaster through no fault of his own and beyond his ability to prevent. This situation produced social security arrangements nationwide in scope.

The world of the mid-twentieth century differs from that of the eighteenth century in another respect. In Franklin's time people lived in small cities, in villages, and on scattered plantations and farms. The individual member of the simple society of those days normally knew his neighbors in terms of the whole pattern of their lives. The eighteenth-century man knew personally the family of his neighbor—grandparents, parents, children. He knew his neighbor's habits as a provider for his household, as a citizen dealing with public affairs, as a member or nonmember of a church. In such a relatively simple society the individual carried weight, and out of this society sprang the basic American values of individual liberty and responsibility. By contrast, a majority of mid-twentieth-century Americans live in some part of a metropolitan complex. In the vast, anonymous metropolis the individual seems to count for little. In a society of specialists the urban individual tends to meet other persons as specialists—the radio repairman, the pharmacist at the drug counter, the teacher of his children, the surgeon who removes an appendix. In this situation the individual adds to his power by working in groups—a labor union, a farm cooperative, a political pressure group. He expresses his regard for his children's school through its parent-teacher's association. He cultivates his special private interests through other voluntary associations—the philatelic club, the camera club, the Audubon Society. Our present more complex society does not dwarf individuality, though for some persons the frustrations it engenders may have that result. Mid-twentieth-century society offers a wider range of areas in which individual fulfillment may be sought and individuality expressed. The American philosopher

Josiah Royce expressed both sides of the coin of modern life in his phrase "We are saved by the community." His "we" referred to independent and autonomous individuals.

Out of this long process of social change have emerged the social values of the American people:

1. The dignity and importance of the individual person. The individual person is, himself, a unique center of power and value. He does not exist for the state. The state, in fact, is no more than an organized community of persons. The state has no being or meaning apart from these persons. The state is an instrument to further the welfare of the persons who compose it. When the state enslaves the persons who compose it, these persons lose that power and dignity which derives ultimately from their humanity.

2. Freedom of thought and action of the individual person. If a person is to have dignity and if his life is to have significance, he must have a large measure of freedom. Nature, of course, sets limitations to that freedom. The prime social limitation lies in the fact that the individual person must manage his behavior so as not to impair the freedom of his fellows.

3. Freedom, and so far as possible equal opportunity, of the individual person to make of his life what he can in accordance with his abilities. The corollary of this concept—the expectation of a status in society that derives from his qualities and achievements.

4. Regard for the group and for group activity as a means to the ends of developing individual personality and of enlarging the possibilities for effective action that has importance for the individual person, resulting in the formation of voluntary associations in extraordinary number and for a wide range of interests.

5. Regard for the family as the basic social institution. Within the family, emphasis on the separate individualities of husband, wife, and children, and the enjoyment by women of equal legal and political rights. Protection in law and custom of the privacy

and mutual loyalty of its members—one spouse may not be compelled to testify in court against the other. The concept that loyalty of its members to the family is a virtue at least equal to loyalty to the state—a conviction evidenced by the complete absence in the United States of efforts by the state to use children or adult members of a family as informers to the state against other members.

6. Regard for work leading to recognizable accomplishment—professional preferment, the accumulation of property —as a normal aspect of the good life. The value expressed in the fact that having a job gives in itself a kind of social status. The tendency to look down upon an idle man unless the idleness is due to infirmity or age. This value expresses the activism in American civilization.

7. Concern for the physical and mental health of the community. This value emerged in the latter half of the nineteenth century when scientific advances enlarged the ability of the doctor to cure disease and made preventive medicine possible. Other scientific advances brought into being rational methods for dealing with mental disorders. This value reached its full expression in public health organizations, regulations, and activities.

8. Regard for voluntary public service by private individuals. This value had its first significant expression in the humanitarian movement of the first half of the nineteenth century. In that period the tradition of humanism of the Enlightenment united with an urge to individual and social betterment in evangelical Protestantism to produce a number of societies and movements to attack social evils and to ameliorate the plight of suffering or oppressed persons. The humanitarian emphasis of the time reached its culmination in the antislavery crusade. The humanitarian movement continued after the Civil War in attempts to deal with the insecurities of a rapidly developing industrialism and with the vice and suffering of the slums of the cities growing swiftly in size as a flood

of immigrants came from abroad. A rough division of function took place between governmental and private efforts to deal with the problem of individual and social maladjustments. Now, in the middle of the twentieth century, municipalities and states provide relief and the arrangements that go under the name of social security. Private agencies work in the field of character-building, rehabilitation of individuals and families, and special training for the handicapped. Beginning in the latter half of the nineteenth century, men of wealth in the United States created a number of foundations, which had large endowments administered in the public interest by professional staffs. The Rockefeller Foundation, the Ford Foundation, and others carry on worldwide activities.

Regard for voluntary public service implies two things. It suggests, on the one hand, the habit that has been developed among citizens of the United States, from the wage earner to the man of wealth, to make regular voluntary contributions of money to institutions and causes which further the general welfare. It implies, on the other hand, willingness on the part of private persons to serve without compensation in the management and promotion of such institutions and causes. The ideal of voluntary public service by private individuals ranks high in the hierarchy of American values.

9. Acceptance of change as a normal aspect of social life and regard for the social sciences as instruments for gaining an understanding of society and for the formulation of improvements. The social sciences are primarily a twentieth-century development in the United States. By the mid-twentieth century, through the knowledge social scientists had acquired and the applications of that knowledge to specific social problems, an important impact on American civilization had been made. In a society in which rapid industrial evolution causes swift and important social changes, the social sciences represent efforts to provide rational solutions to complex and urgent problems.

Science in American Values

The English colonies that ultimately grew into the United States were, save one, founded in the seventeenth century when modern science came into being. From the beginning of the eighteenth century, institutions of higher learning in America gave increasing attention to mathematics and to the natural sciences. In this same century the Enlightenment, emphasizing reason, profoundly affected American thought. The Newtonian conception of a mechanistic universe came to provide the background for much of American philosophy.

In the nineteenth century, Americans made an impressive number of practical technological advances—the steamboat, the sewing machine, the telegraph, the telephone, and the incandescent lamp, to mention only a few. In the same century, American universities and museums of natural history made important contributions to the development of pure science—in particular in the fields of geology, paleontology, botany, and thermo-dynamics. The government of the United States, through such agencies as the National Observatory, the Bureau of Standards, the Smithsonian Institution, the U.S. Geological Survey, and the research bureaus of the Department of Agriculture, contributed significantly to the accumulation of scientific knowledge and its application to the problems confronting American society.

By the time the century had passed its zenith, the officials of government and the intelligent American public had achieved a new perspective in social thinking. They had come to understand that the arrangements of society rest on a body of knowledge (the accumulated knowledge of the natural sciences, of technology, and of the social sciences) and that evolution in this substructure is the primary cause for social change. Americans, as they stood on the threshold of a new space age, had reached the conviction that the continued progress of the Republic, in fact its very survival, depends upon determined and unremitting efforts to push out the boundaries of all knowledge. To this end the government appropriated vast sums for basic research.

The values of science as they have emerged in American life include the following concepts:

1. Regard for rationality—the critical approach to the phenomena of nature and of society, coupled with the effort to reduce these phenomena to ever more consistent, orderly, and generalized forms of understanding.

2. The conviction that man must dare to unlock the secrets of nature to the extent that his abilities permit.

3. The conviction that man must accept and not shirk the moral responsibility for the use of whatever new power increased knowledge brings to him.

4. The understanding that the method of science, combining precise reasoning with accurate observation and controlled experiment, can achieve new knowledge when and only when it conforms to an ethical code, a code that might almost be described as the laws of creative thought. These laws are stated in 5, 6, and 7 below.

5. The scholar who seeks new knowledge must have freedom to explore, to reason on the basis of discovered fact, and to express his conclusions.

6. In communicating what he has found, the scholar must be faithful to the truth he has discovered; he must describe honestly what he has observed or found by calculation.

7. The scholar must approach the solution of problems with objectivity, a willingness to accept evidence and to reject disproved hypotheses, no matter what the consequences.

8. Regard for the application of scientific knowledge through technology to the affairs of life. Among the values relating to science, regard for technology was primary among Americans until after World War II. The scientific achievements in the 1950s,

however, brought home to the citizens of the United States the fact that perhaps even national survival depends on pushing out the boundaries of knowledge on all fronts. The huge sums that the federal government has made available for basic research give evidence that Americans have achieved a new perspective.

The prominent role of the natural and social sciences in the United States and their profound influence upon American society have resulted in a growing insistence on the part of an expanding proportion of the populace that in private and public affairs evidence must be presented before conclusions can be drawn and the decisions must be based on reality rather than wishful thinking. Unless such objectivity characterizes the people as a whole, government by the people cannot succeed.

Traditionally, the advance of science has depended upon the free flow of information concerning new discoveries among scientists without regard to national boundaries. The conditions of the twentieth century have put obstacles in the way of such exchange of knowledge. American scientists have been disturbed by these limitations on the operation of the basic canons governing creative scientific thought. Although recognizing the requirements of national security in the matter of secrecy in some research and in certain government contracts, they strive to keep classified scientific material limited to that which is vital to the safety of the nation. Their goal is the continuation of science to advance with a minimum of man-made impediments into the boundless area of the unknown.

Values in the American Economy

The transplanted Englishmen who established the North American colonies in the seventeenth century founded their economy on the principles of free enterprise and private property. In the simple society of the seventeenth-century settlements, the entrepreneur—as fur trader with the Indians, as merchant adventurer in the West Indian trade, or as producer of tobacco for sale on a Virginia plantation—became a central and important figure. Colonial economy was primarily agrarian. The typical husbandman, however, was not the southern planter nor the large landowner of the North, but rather the small and independent farmer who worked his land with his own hands. The family got its food, shelter, and clothing from its piece of land cleared from the forest. For the great majority of colonial Americans, the economy was little more than a subsistence economy. Technology was in the handicraft stage.

From the first settlements Americans considered economic well-being the foundation of the general well-being of both individual and community life. The religion of the Puritans emphasized work as against sloth and saving as against extravagant consumption. The emphasis on work and saving fitted the needs of a people who were expanding westward across an empty continent and a situation in which labor was normally in short supply in the light of the tasks to be accomplished.

At the end of the eighteenth century, the basic machines of England's Industrial Revolution, together with the factory system, started Americans on the road to an industrial civilization. Individual proprietors or partnerships owned and managed the first factories. In the second half of the nineteenth century, entrepreneurs used the limited liability corporation to bring together the capital, labor, and machines necessary for any particular type of production. The corporation remained in the twentieth century the primary form of organization of enterprises in the American economy.

In the nineteenth century, railroads were built by private companies, though the federal government gave grants of money and land to the builders of the transcontinental lines. Most of the canals in that time were created by state funds. The federal government maintained the postal system, and municipalities normally provided for the needs of cities for water. But these and a few other public undertakings were small in comparison with the vast extent of private enterprise.

By World War I American civilization had left behind the agrarianism that had been dominant until the middle of the nineteenth century. After that conflict a rapidly evolving industrialism created new wealth and a new mode of life. Giant corporations, such as General Motors and General Electric, took a leading position in the American economy. Giant unions, such as the United Steel Workers and the United Auto Workers, came into being as a countervailing force. In the twentieth century, public enterprise has taken the additional form of the production of hydroelectric power and of atomic power, though it has far from preempted these fields. With industrial civilization came new insecurities—industrial accidents, unemployment, insufficient housing, the need for income on the part of the worker retired from his job for age. In the middle decades of the twentieth century, big government appeared to meet the needs of the nation as it went forward in an industrial age and in an epoch characterized by revolutions and wars. The government assumed responsibility for holding the economy stable (as against periods of boom and depression), for upholding employment, for measures to provide social security to the citizen, for support for agriculture against prices for commodities too low to enable the farmers to maintain solvency. The economy became a blend of public and private enterprise. Within it private enterprise balanced public regulation and assistance. The complex of values that has emerged to guide this economy includes the following concepts:

1. Work on the part of the individual person has been valued since the theology of the seventeenth-century Puritans sanctified it. A job, no matter how humble, gives honorable status to an individual and is the normal way of life.

2. Economic well-being of the individual person is valued not

only as the cornerstone of a sound economy but as the essential foundation for a full and rounded individual life. Economic well-being frequently is defined in very simple terms in a material sense. Poverty, as in certain religious orders, is not an important value.

3. The sanctity of contract and respect for property are valued as the foundation for orderly and dependable economic relations.

4. Production of goods is valued as a prerequisite to economic well-being. The drive toward more efficient and increasing production is one of the most important in the American economy.

5. Private enterprise is valued because it gives opportunity for the creative potentialities of the entrepreneur or of corporate management, because it gives the entrepreneur the largest measure of freedom in working out the destinies of the particular concern, and because the opportunities of sharing in the profits resulting from successful management provides a stimulus for individual effort.

6. The profit system is valued because only where there are profits can private enterprise long continue. The profit system is modified or limited by government entry into the economy through laws dealing with manufacturing and price competition, such as those dealing with monopolies, unfair methods of competition, and rate fixing for public utilities; laws dealing with the quality of products sold; laws governing the conditions of work in mines, factories, and service undertakings; tax laws that appropriate for the general use a considerable percentage of the profits of private industry; and government operation of certain enterprises to prevent abuses by private monopoly or near monopoly.

7. The economic well-being of the community (from the local community to the nation) is valued for the same reason that the economic well-being of individual persons is valued and for the following other reasons: The economy can function successfully only so long as the mass of the people enjoy a considerable measure of economic well-being; production depends upon consumption; the economy can operate properly only when the con-

suming public can purchase the fruits of production; wage policies by private enterprise are conditioned by the need for economic well-being of the community because the ability to consume for most of the population derives from wages and salaries. This same need conditions governmental policies having to do with credit and in particular with the distribution of the national wealth through taxes on profits and through graduated income and estate taxes. The graduated income tax has made the concentration of a great percentage of the national income in the hands of a few persons impossible. A prime motive of the income tax is to maintain the economic well-being of the community.

8. Social security for the individual person is valued. It takes the form of insurance plans under the auspices of the state. It applies to the unemployed, to the industrially insured, and to the aged. Private and cooperative social security is valued for two reasons. It preserves to a degree the economic well-being of the individual, with all of the implications of that goal. It helps to maintain the purchasing power of the mass of the people and so serves the goal of the economic well-being of the community.

9. The principle of assistance by the state to certain economic groups is valued because it furthers the economic prosperity of the community. The state provides price supports for some agricultural commodities so that the farmers may continue to function normally as producers and as consumers. The state sets a minimum wage rate so that wage earners may continue to function as consumers. These are the economic reasons. Behind these are the reasons of humanity expressed in the goal (before considered) of the economic well-being of the individual person.

10. In spite of the fact that the policy of price supports by the government for agricultural products prevents competition among producing farmers from bringing down prices below certain levels, Americans value the principle and practice of competition in the production and distribution of goods and services. This approval is specifically expressed in laws forbidding monopoly,

save in certain fields such as the telephone. Americans fear that monopoly power in private hands may lead to exploitation of the community. The states and the federal government have created agencies for the regulation of monopolies that are inherently desirable.

11. In the production of goods, rationalization and mechanization are valued. Mass production of goods, such as automobiles or refrigerators, brings down the price of the individual unit to a point where it can be purchased by the mass of the people. The result is the furthering of the economic well-being of the individual person and of the community.

12. The principle of collective bargaining is valued because it enables the worker to negotiate with the employer on more nearly equal terms and, as a result, have a voice in the formulation of policies of vital importance to his life as a workman.

13. Opportunity for the individual employee to rise in the managerial hierarchy of an enterprise through promotions based on efficiency is valued for two reasons: It provides for the mobilization of the maximum ability in the management of the enterprise; and it expresses the larger American ideal of giving the individual person the opportunity to make of his life what he can.

14. Americans value government in the roles not only of maintaining order and administering justice, but also in those aiding stable economic growth and preventing excessive economic inequalities.

The foregoing goals can be isolated and analyzed each by itself, but their full meaning can be understood only when they are viewed as parts of a single complex of interrelated and mutually supporting values. Taken together they provide the ultimate controls over the drive toward ruthless competition of predatory use of power present in many persons who have achieved strategic positions in the economy. Because such drives are inherent in human nature, they can never be completely curbed. Long experience in dealing with individual or corporate ruthlessness has established in American thought the percept: Constant watchfulness is the price of general prosperity.

In the middle of the twentieth century, as the machine increased in importance in the American economy, the work-week of the wage earner grew shorter. Leisure increased. Leisure gave opportunity for "do-it-yourself" tasks of maintenance and improvement about the home, more chance for trips in the family car, greater opportunities for pursuing individual or group hobbies and for participation in or attendance upon sports. Providing small tools and supplies for do-it-yourself activities became an aspect of some importance in the economy. In many communities throughout the nation, handicrafts—weaving, woodworking, ceramics, rug-making, copper and silver work—achieved a high level of artistic quality. Many craftsmen turn out their creations as a vocation, but more find in handicrafts a pleasant leisure-time activity.

The arrangements of the American economy make it possible for the great majority of citizens of the United States to enjoy both as a community and as individual persons a high level of economic well-being. This high standard cannot be explained by merely pointing to the natural resources of the nation. Some of these are sadly depleted in spite of conservation movements. The phenomenon is explained rather by the complex of economic values and technologies operating together in a single economy that functions in a realistic sense to utilize these resources for the general welfare. The mixed American economy may be accurately described as a general welfare economy. It is a blend of private enterprise and the undertakings of a general welfare state. It is neither classically "capitalist" nor "socialist." It blends basic reliance upon individual initiative with group action and governmental initiative —when necessary—to insure the achievement of social ideals. Private enterprise distributes decision-making throughout the economy, in contrast to the concentration of decision-making in the hands of the highest echelon of governmental officials in a totalitarian command economy.

The Arts in American Life

In the main, the arts in American life in the past and in the present derive from the artistic tradition of Western civilization. But the art of Asia, particularly the visual arts of Japan, has also contributed to American architecture, especially on the West Coast, and more recently to crafts and painting. From the first half of the nineteenth century, the religious thought of Asia has affected American literature. Since the beginning of American history, however, each successive frontier produced its own folk songs and oral folk literature. In the older and more settled regions, each generation created its quasi-folk songs, such as Stephen Foster's "Old Folks at Home," first published in 1851 and, in the century which followed, one of the most frequently republished and widely sung pieces in the English language. In the twentieth century, an indigenous art took its place beside that derived from tradition. In architecture, in literature, and, since the mid-twentieth century, in modern abstract painting, American artists blazed new trails and made distinctive contributions to the art of the world.

Although interest in and appreciation of the beautiful were present in American life from the first settlements, the development of the fine arts was hampered in the seventeenth century by the hard conditions of life in frontier settlements expanding westward into the wilderness. Moreover, in relatively more populous New England, the Puritans opposed all theater and most of the other arts as either immoral or frivolous.

In the eighteenth-century colonial cities that grew up on the harbors of the Atlantic coast from Boston, Massachusetts, to Charleston, South Carolina, and on the plantations of Virginia and

Carolina lowlands, a more polished civilization replaced the cruder life of earlier years. Eighteenth-century colonials, many of whom possessed substantial means, created public and private buildings in the Georgian style that represented so high a level of artistic achievement as to be appreciated and imitated in the United States two centuries later. In New England the Georgian churches built by descendants of the first Puritans became a notable artistic expression of that period. In the latter half of the eighteenth century, painting, particularly portrait painting of high standard, developed to such an extent that the features of the leading figures in the Revolution and the writing of the Constitution have been familiar to all succeeding generations.

The theater, presenting mostly imported plays, began to flourish in the second quarter of the nineteenth century. It produced in Edwin Booth an actor-artist numbered among the greats of all times. European music brought to America, particularly by German and Scandinavian immigrants, became important at the same time as the theater. The high point in artistic achievement of early America was reached in the literary flowering of the second third of the nineteenth century. This contributed to American and Western tradition the work of Poe, Hawthorne, Melville, Emerson, Thoreau, and Whitman.

In 1862, the year in which Thoreau died, Americans, suffering through a second year of fratricidal war, stood on the threshold of vast social changes. In the last third of the nineteenth century, the old agrarian civilization gave way to a swiftly marching industrialism. An immigrant flood brought an ethnic revolution. Universities, some new and some rising out of older colleges, achieved maturity, and a few took their place among the world's great centers of learning. In these years of swift increase in the national wealth, art benefited. Many wealthy Americans began to acquire works of art on a large scale both for private collections and public art museums. Today most of these important art collections have passed into our museums, some of which rival the great public art collections of Europe and Asia. The Metropolitan Museum of Art and the Museum of Modern Art at New York City, the Boston Museum of Fine Arts, the Art Institute at Chicago, and the National Gallery of Art and the Freer Gallery of Art at Washington, D.C., possess and display an extraordinary variety of treasures from all the continents. But many distinguished museums also exist in other cities of the United States. Organizations of professional and amateur artists arrange periodic art exhibitions and art festivals in our larger cities and many of our smaller ones. Similarly, our large universities and colleges give active support to art, music, and theater, as well as to literature and poetry. There are also many professional schools for training students in the arts, architecture, music, and drama. The one-way transportation of culture from Europe to America during the earlier history of the country has been replaced by a two-way international cultural traffic.

For America the first half of the twentieth century, disturbed by two world wars, was a creative era. Beside the emergence of the industrial giants and the evolution of the general welfare state must be put the achievements of the natural sciences and the social sciences. And with these changes came innovations in the arts of scarcely less magnitude.

The pioneering orchestras of the middle of the nineteenth century inaugurated a movement that put an orchestra in every important city. Through these and many other musical organizations, Americans achieved distinguished performance of music. At the same time out of different corners of the nation came an indigenous music. Negro spirituals first rose in the days of slavery and have become a distinctive folk music. In the twentieth century, Negroes, beginning in New Orleans and St. Louis, originated and developed jazz and the blues. As the century progressed, this indigenous music—in the hands of such masters as Louis Armstrong—underwent evolution until it achieved at its best art forms with classical overtones. In the middle decades of the twentieth century, jazz made an important impact beyond the national borders. Charles Ives pioneered in a style of serious music which by the middle of the century had produced a distinguished literature in which tradition and innovation blended. Indigenous music entered the theater to produce the opera "Porgy and Bess" and such musicals as "Oklahoma" and "My Fair Lady." The mass acceptance of hi-fi and stereophonic recordings has brought music of superior quality into American homes in a significant way. In the theater Eugene O'Neill was merely the first among a mid-twentieth-century group of playwrights who made the drama a force in American life. Architecture in the same century covered the entire spectrum from reproducing forms as old as those of Greece and Rome to free and infinitely varied experimentation with steel, concrete, and glass. Frank Lloyd Wright was only one among several whose buildings were known beyond the borders of the nation. Among the most important and beautiful material monuments created by the age were the skyscrapers, bridges, and multilane highways to be found in all parts of the country. After World War I an outpouring of American letters added to the Western heritage the poetry of Frost, Eliot, Pound, and Sandburg, and the prose of Hemingway and Faulkner.

In this twentieth century of growth and change and war, the American people expressed themselves as never before through the arts. Mass communication brought art to the great audience. In America, whose people were a blend of many ethnic strains and where social classes had fluid and uncertain boundaries, an art that expressed the emotions and tastes of the masses of the people found expression in music, in the cinema, and later in the entertainments of television. It took its place beside the elite art derived from the artistic tradition of the West. But there was as little clash between the two as between American social classes. Partisans of elite art enjoyed the musicals and even followed the comments on life made by the comic strips in the daily press. The so-called masses in great numbers visited the museums of traditional and of modern art and supported the orchestras of their public schools and their cities. In this mingling in the arts of the appeal to the elite and to the great audience, both the fine creation and the mediocre performance stood side by side. There is a serious problem in offering art and culture to the mass audience in finding the appropriate level at which the masses can participate without debasing or watering down artistic excellence. This problem particularly affects TV programs and the motion picture industry. In recent years the book industry has been successful in marketing large-scale editions of high-class books through inexpensive paperback editions. The importance of criticism to maintain standards of excellence is increasingly recognized in university teaching, in scholarly and popular journals, and in the press.

Out of the varied expressions of the arts as they have evolved through the years have emerged certain values. They include the following values:

1. Regard for the creation and presentation of music, reflected in the multiplication of composers, the growth of musical organizations, and the vast importance of recorded music.

2. Regard for the collection of and making available to the public in museums painting, sculpture, and the crafts, both classical and contemporary.

3. Regard for the quality of design in the artifacts of everyday life.

4. Regard for creative literature as an instrument for the fuller and deeper understanding of life.

5. Regard for the drama and the dance as presented in stage, film, and TV as instruments for enriching human life.

6. Regard for tradition and for innovation in painting, sculpture, and the crafts and for popular and mature participation in these arts.

7. Regard for tradition and innovation, together with the principles of form and function, in the architecture of a nation building

to meet the needs of an increasing population and a swiftly evolving civilization.

8. Regard for criticism by scholars and specialists in the various arts to encourage discrimination by the public in appraising performance and recognizing excellence.

Unlike Europe, where museums, music, and the theater receive substantial governmental support, in the United States the traditional relationship of the federal government and art is one of separation. Private means support all the arts in this country. Signs in the middle of the twentieth century, however, pointed to the beginnings of a concern for art on the part of the federal government.

Values in International Relations

American values in the field of international relations come out of something more than a century and a half of experience on the part of the United States as a member of the society of nations. The Republic became an independent nation at a time when major tensions existed in Europe, particularly between Britain and France. As a result of these tensions, the United States was not only enabled to establish its policies without fear of imperialist aggression against it, but in 1803 was able to purchase from Napoleon a vast territory which that ruler feared might fall into the hands of Britain as a result of the control of the seas by the British fleet. Until the end of the Napoleonic Wars in 1815, European divisions enabled the American people to establish firmly the foundations of the nation.

From 1815 to 1914, Europe remained at peace with the exception of the brief wars that brought the Italian and German nations into existence and the Crimean War. In this century of stable balance of power in Europe, the United States based its foreign policy on President George Washington's Farewell Address urging aloofness from Old World politics, on the Monroe Doctrine warning Europeans not to interfere with the new nations of America, on the principle of equal opportunities for trade among all nations, and on the recognition of the equal sovereignty under international law of all *de facto* states, with preference for settlement of disputes by impartial arbitration. These policies were generally favored by Great Britain, with whom, alone among the European powers, the United States had important relations. Sheltered by oceans dominated by British seapower, Americans were free to direct their thoughts and activities to the occupation of the wilderness in the western half of the North American continent and to the extension of the national power over an area larger than Europe. In the nineteenth century, the United States expanded through treaties with France, Spain, Great Britain, Mexico, and Russia. The American nation purchased Florida from Spain, and Alaska from Russia. Both have become states in the Union. The treaty with Britain divided the wilderness in the far Northwest where nationals from both countries had settled. The treaty with Mexico terminated a war in which Mexico was defeated and ceded to the United States the broad territory then known as New Mexico and California, for which the United States paid $15,000,000. At the end of the nineteenth century, a rebellion in the Spanish colony of Cuba led to a short war for the independence of that country between the United States and Spain. As a result of this conflict, the United States occupied Cuba and took possession of the Spanish colonies of Puerto Rico, Guam, and the Philippines for which $20,000,000 was paid. After a few years American forces were withdrawn from Cuba, and Cuba became an independent nation. The period of dependence was longer for the Philippines, but it also became independent in 1946. Soon after World War II the people of Puerto Rico adopted a constitution which was approved by the Congress of the United States, under which they elect their own officials and enjoy autonomy in local affairs. Puerto Ricans are citizens of the United States and subject to the jurisdiction of that nation in external affairs.

In 1917 the United States, after nearly three years of neutrality, became involved in World War I over the issue of neutral rights, protection of democracy, and security of the United States against a German-dominated Europe. The American reinforcement of the armies of the Allies brought about the defeat of the Central Powers. After 1918 the United States refused to join the League of Nations established at the initiative of President Woodrow Wilson as the appropriate means to make the world safe for democracies such as the United States. Domestic politics, senatorial jealousy of presidential power, and fear of involving the nation in future European wars accounted for this decision, which was supported by slightly over one-third of the Senate. (Ratification of a treaty requires under the Constitution a two-thirds affirmative vote in the Senate.) As a result of the failure of the United States to become a member of the League of Nations, the American people reverted to isolationism, which continued to dominate their thinking until the eve of World War II. The federal government, however, participated in financial settlements in Europe and in disarmament and antiwar negotiations and cooperated with the League of Nations, especially after the advent of President Franklin D. Roosevelt and Secretary of State Cordell Hull, both committed to Wilsonian internationalism.

For the United States, World War II began dramatically and tragically as a war for survival. During its course, American military power appeared on all the continents and in all the oceans. When the fighting was over, the United States did not seek or acquire any new territory. In place of following the time-honored maxim, "To the victors belong the spoils," America undertook to bind up the wounds of war. Through the Marshall Plan the United

States offered aid to the war-ravaged nations of Europe. The initial offer included the U.S.S.R., but that nation spurned it and coerced its new satellites into a similar policy. Later, the United States brought technical aid and assistance under President Harry Truman's Point Four proposal to many less-developed countries. While possessing a monopoly of the atom bomb, the United States proposed to internationalize control of atomic energy under the United Nations, a suggestion that failed because of the objections of the U.S.S.R. As international tensions multiplied in the postwar world, the United States assumed farflung responsibilities to contain the outward thrust of Communist imperialism, with increased realization, after China had become Communist and Russia had acquired atomic weapons and intercontinental ballistic missiles, that peaceful relations must be maintained among all nations, however varied their ideologies.

Out of this long and varied experience as a member of the society of nations have come the values by which the United States seeks to guide its dealings with foreign states. They include the following concepts:

1. The principle that changes in the relations between nation-states be accomplished by peaceful means alone—the rejection of violence as an instrument of policy.

2. The principle of national sovereignty under international law. Because Americans value this principle for their own country, they regard as axiomatic the right of other nations, small or large, to security of their territory and the determination of their own form of government and economy and of their own foreign and domestic policy. This concept is a projection into the area of international relations and an extension to nations of that basic value in American thought; namely, the free and responsible individual person.

3. The value of collective security within an organization of

nation-states has been increasingly recognized in the twentieth century, superseding the older isolationism. As the individual person is a unit in a society and is conditioned by that society, the independent nation is a unit in a society of nation-states and must accept those limitations on independence of action which derive from that fact. These limitations have become increasingly important as improvement in transportation and communication have crowded the nations close together. A corollary to the value of collective security is the understanding that no nation can enjoy prosperity in isolation, that, in general, prosperity in neighboring nations reinforces prosperity at home. Out of this understanding has come in the United States the value that emphasizes the well-being of the community of nations through arrangements for mutual aid. These have included bilateral arrangements between the Republic and another power, but the United States has increasingly participated in the multilateral arrangements through the United Nations, UNESCO, the World Bank, and other international organizations.

4. The observance of international law and international commitments formally undertaken. The honoring of treaties is a basic responsibility of a free nation. It is the prerequisite of orderly relations among nations and of any significant world organization of nation-states.

5. The use of international adjudication to settle legal disputes. American Presidents have urged formal commitments to this effect since 1896, and the Senate has often agreed to submit specific disputes to adjudication.

6. The concept that free nations should practice neighborliness and that the stronger and more advanced among them should respond to requests for help, particularly from peoples struggling to escape from inherited poverty.

7. The concept that government should encourage and support cultural exchange among peoples, on the ground that increased

understanding among diverse civilizations and mutual appreciation of their art and their values further the cause of fellowship among men of good will, and so of peace.

The foregoing principles represent the values which the nation tried to use as a pole star by which to steer the course of foreign policy through both calm and stormy seas. As in every area of human endeavor, disparities between ideal and practice appeared in different places and at different times. When such deviations occurred, the values described served as the basis of criticism intended to return policy to its proper course. The responsibilities of leadership in the defense of the free world against totalitarian authoritarianism, whether of the Left or of the Right, of human rights and the self-determination of peoples against totalitarian dictator-states and against foreign aggression and intervention brought to the United States dilemmas that could not be avoided. The tensions of the Cold War continued year after year, but Americans did not lose faith in the possibility of a genuine peace. Though the night was long, they held fast to the hope of a dawn that would break when peoples could communicate through the free flow of ideas with one another, when governments of all important powers would exist to reinforce the dignity of men, and when the philosophy of the nations would recognize that a cold, deterministic materialism can neither describe nor contain the soaring and invincible human spirit.

Appreciation

I wish to express my thanks for aid rendered by the United States National Commission's Subcommittee on Traditional Values in Modern Life in India and in the United States, consisting of the following members: Henry R. Hope, chairman, Fine Arts Department, Indiana University; Eugene E. Barnett, National Council of Churches of Christ in the U.S.A.; Robert Blum, former president, Asia Foundation; Paul J. Braisted, president, Edward Hazen Foundation: Lewis M. Hoskins, former executive secretary, American Friends Service Committee; James Laughlin, president, Intercultural Publications, Inc.; Shannon B. McCune, former acting president, University of Massachusetts; Donald H. Shively, Department of Oriental Languages, University of California; Frank M. Snowden, Jr., dean, College of Liberal Arts, Howard University.

In addition, my thanks go to the following persons who read and criticized this essay: W. Norman Brown, Ralph E. Cleland, Norman Cousins, Merle Curti, William S. Dix, Frank L. Fernbach, Arthur B. Foye, Chadbroune Gilpatric, Ernest S. Griffith, John W. Hanes, Selig H. Harrison, M. Jacques Havet, Fajendea Kunnan, David G. Mandelbaum, A. E. Manell, Albert H. Marckwardt, Kenneth W. Morgan, Herbert J. Muller, Chester L. Neudling, William A. Noyes, George E. Probst, R. Salat, Paul C. Sherbert, and Richard L. Watson, Jr. They have contributed much to whatever excellence the essay may have. They are not to be held responsible for its defects.

I am especially grateful to Max McCullough at whose suggestion the work was begun, to Quincy Wright for many contributions to the text, and to William C. Mithoefer, Jr., and Lois Haase of the Secretariat, the United States National Commission for UNESCO, for criticisms and suggestions and for help in expediting the completion of the work.

R.H.G.

A Selected Bibliography of the Writings of Ralph Henry Gabriel

The following list grew from the files of the author himself. It was checked against the catalogs and derivative source books in the Library of Congress where Ruth Freitag, of the General Reference and Bibliography Division, gave helpful counsel as to sources, form, and order. No effort was made to include book reviews. In some cases separate printings were not noted, although major editions of all works have been listed. Because this is a retrospective listing appearing near the end of a long and varied career, it was decided to reproduce it in chronological order, thus stressing the intellectual biography of a scholar whose interests and competences reflect a continuing growth.

An asterisk preceding the entry identifies it as part of the present collection.

R.H.W.
April 1973

"Geographic Influences in the Development of the Menhaden Fishery on the Eastern Coast of the United States," *The Geographical Review* 10 (August 1920): 91-100.

The Evolution of Long Island, a Story of Land and Sea. New Haven: Yale University Press, 1921. 194p. (Reprinted, Port Washington, L.I.: Ira J. Friedman, 1968.)

"Farmer in the Commonwealth," *North American Review* 213 (May 1921): 577-586.

"The General Course in United States History and the Liberal Arts College," *Historical Outlook* 12 (October 1921): 237-239.

(With Dumas Malone, Frederick J. Manning.) *An Outline of United States History for Use in the General Course in Yale College*. New Haven: Yale University Press, 1921. 28p.

(Part of a symposium with Beverley W. Bond, Jr., and Arthur M. Schlesinger, conducted in New Haven, December 1922.) "The Method of the General Course in American History," *Historical Outlook* 14 (March 1923): 93-98.

"The *Chronicles of America* and the Teaching of History," *Ohio History Teachers Journal*, No. 34 (May 1924): 447-452.

(Edited with a foreword.) Charles R. Brown, et al. *Christianity and Modern Thought*. New Haven: Yale University Press, 1924. 196p.

(With Arthur B. Darling.) *The Yale Course of Home Study Based on The Chronicles of America*. New Haven: Yale University Press, 1924. 301p. (Reprinted in 1926 as Vol. 26 in *The Chronicles of America* series.)

(General editor and author of a foreword for each volume.) *The Pageant of America*. 15 vols. New Haven: Yale University Press, 1925-1929.

(Edited and with additional essays by Henri L. Bourdin and Stanley T. Williams.) St. John de Crèvecoeur. *Sketches of Eighteenth-Century America, More "Letters of an American Farmer."* New Haven: Yale University Press, 1925. 342p.

Toilers of Land and Sea, American Agriculture and Fisheries. New Haven: Yale University Press, 1926. 340p. (*Pageant of America*, Vol. 3)

(With William Wood.) *The Winning of Freedom*. New Haven: Yale University Press, 1927. 366p. (*Pageant of America*, Vol. 6)

(With William Wood.) *In Defense of Liberty*. New Haven: Yale University Press, 1928. 370p. (*Pageant of America*, Vol. 7)

The Lure of the Frontier, a Story of Race Conflict. New Haven: Yale University Press, 1929. 327p. (*Pageant of America*, Vol. 2)

(Foreword.) Walter Stemmons. *Connecticut Agricultural College, a*

History. Storrs, Conn.: Connecticut Agricultural College, 1931. 258p.

"Crèvecoeur, an Orange County Paradox," *New York State Historical Association Journal* 12 (1931): 45-55.

(With Mabel B. Casner.) *Exploring American History.* New York: Harcourt Brace, 1931. 787p. This textbook appeared in many printings and editions, including such title variations as *The Rise of American Democracy* (1938), *The Story of American Democracy* (1942 and after; the 1955 edition under this title carried an introduction by Carl Sandburg), *The Story of the American Nation* (1962).

(Edited, with an essay on the manuscript.) Sarah Royce. *A Frontier Lady, Recollections of the Gold Rush and Early California.* Foreword by Katharine Royce. New Haven: Yale University Press, 1932. 144p.

The Founding of Holyoke, 1848, a Newcomen Address. Princeton: Princeton University Press, 1936. 23p. (Delivered at Greenfield, Mass., October 8, 1936.)

(Edited with Harry R. Warfel and Stanley T. Williams.) *The American Mind, Selections from the Literature of the United States.* New York: American Book Co., 1937. 155p. (This sourcebook has been reprinted and revised several times, the latest printing, 2 vols., in 1963.)

"Remarks by the Chairman." In *Approaches to American Social History*, edited by William E. Linglebach, p. 8-13. New York: Appleton-Century, 1937. (From a general session of the American Historical Association, Providence, R.I., 1936.)

*"Constitutional Democracy, a Nineteenth-Century Faith." In *The Constitution Reconsidered*, edited by Conyers Read, p. 247-258 New York: Columbia University Press, 1938. (Revised edition with a new preface by Richard B. Morris. New York: Harper & Row, 1968.)

"Early Yale Inventors—David Bushnell, Samuel Finley Breese Morse and Eli Whitney Blake." In *Inventors and Engineers of Old New Haven*, edited by Richard S. Kirby, p. 25-36. New Haven: New Haven Colony Historical Society, 1939.

"Memorial Day Address" (on the meaning to America of the fall of France), New Haven *Journal Courier*, May 31, 1940.

American Democracy in the World Crisis. Norton, Mass.: Periwinkle Press, 1940. 18p. (Prepared as the concluding paper in a social science symposium, Wheaton College, October 5, 1940.)

The Course of American Democratic Thought. New York: Ronald Press,

1940. 452p. Revised edition, 1956, 508p. Also published in Berlin: Duncker & Humbolt, 1951, as *Die Enwicklung des Demokratischen Gedankens.*

Elias Boudinot, Cherokee, and his America. Norman: University of Oklahoma Press, 1941. 190p.

"Democracy: Retrospect and Prospect," *American Journal of Sociology* 48 (November 1942): 411-418.

Main Currents in American History. New York: Appleton-Century, 1942. 190p. (These lectures for servicemen were reprinted as Part III, "American History and the Constitution," in *School of the Citizen Soldier*, 1942, and *School of the Citizen Sailor*, 1943.)

"Planning for the Post-War World," *Current History*, n.s. 4 (March 1943): 2-3.

"Looking Backward at 1943," *Nation's Business* 31 (May 1943): 80 *et passim.*

"American Experience with Military Government," *American Political Science Review* 37 (June 1943): 417-438. (The author lectured at the War Department School of Military Government from May 1943 until it closed in February 1946.)

"American Experience with Military Government," *American Historical Review* 49 (July 1944): 630-643.

"Philippines," *Yale Review* 34 (September 1944): 14-26.

*"Our Spiritual Heritage, the Moral and Religious Foundations of American Life." In *Education and the Faith of America*, p. 1-13. Brooklyn, N.Y.: Packer Collegiate Institute, 1945. (Reprinted as Hazen Pamphlet No. 14, *Spiritual Origins of American Culture.* Haddam, Conn.: The Edward W. Hazen Foundation, 1945. 17p. It had originally been read before a conference on Education and the Faith of America at the Packer Collegiate Institute on April 12, 1945. The author reports that, immediately following his address, came the shocking word of Franklin D. Roosevelt's sudden death.)

"The American Labor Movement Today," *The Australian Quarterly* 18 (December 1946): 89-98.

*"The Enlightenment Tradition." In *Wellsprings of the American Spirit*, edited by P. Ernest Johnson, p. 39-47. New York: Institute for Religious and Social Studies, 1948. (Originally an address at the Jewish Theological Seminary of America, New York City.)

"Mark Twain." In Robert E. Spiller, et al. *Literary History of the United*

States, Chapter 56, II, p. 917-939 . New York: Macmillan, 1949. (This work has appeared in several printings and editions since.)

*"Evangelical Religion and Popular Romanticism in Early Nineteenth-Century America," *Church History* 19 (March 1950): 34-47.

*"Thomas Jefferson and Twentieth-Century Rationalism," *Virginia Quarterly Review* 26 (Summer 1950): 321-335.

(Part of a symposium.) "The Library of Congress and American Scholarship," *American Library Association Bulletin* 44 (October 1950): 339-359.

"Ideas in History," *History of Education Journal* 2 (Summer 1951): 97-106.

(General Editor.) *Library of Congress Series in American Civilization*. 12 vols. Cambridge: Harvard University Press, 1951-1964.

(Edited with an introduction.) *The Federalist: Hamilton, Madison and Jay on the Constitution; Selections from the Federalist Papers*. New York: Liberal Arts Press, 1954. 235p. (Translated as *The Federalist. El Derecho de Gobernar*. Buenos Aires: Editorial Agora, 1957.)

"New England" entry in *Encyclopedia Britannica*. Chicago: William Benton, since 1954 and through the 1973 editions. (Volume and page numbers vary; 4p. in length.)

*"Religion in American Life." In *National Policies for Education, Health and Social Services*, edited by James E. Russell, p. 413-431. New York: Doubleday, 1955. (Columbia University Bicentennial Series.)

*"Nationalism and the Atom," *The Virginia Quarterly Review* 33 (Fall 1957): 539-548.

A Journey to Britain, Our Troubled Ally. New Haven: New Haven Colony Historical Society, 1957. 9p. (A paper read before the Society on November 19, 1956.)

Religion and Learning at Yale, the Church of Christ in the College and University, 1757-1957. New Haven: Yale University Press, 1958. 271p.

*"The Cold War and Changes in American Thought," *The Virginia Quarterly Review* 35 (Winter 1959): 53-63.

(With William H. Hartley and Elliott H. Kone.) Editor. *Chronicles of America Filmstrips*. New Haven: Yale University Press Film Service, 1959. (Fifteen strips.)

Traditional Values in American Life. Washington, D.C.: U.S. National

Commission for UNESCO, 1960. 40p. (Reprinted, New York: Harcourt Brace & World, 1963; also Tokyo: Nan' un-do, 1964, with notes in Japanese by Tateo Takechi and Masao Kunihiro.)

"History and the American Past." In *American Perspectives, the National Self-Image in the Twentieth Century*, edited by Robert E. Spiller and Eric Labaree, p. 1-16. Cambridge: Harvard University Press, 1961. (A volume in the *Library of Congress Series in American Civilization*.)

"Ideas and Culture in the Twentieth Century." In *Interpreting and Teaching American History*, edited by William H. Cartwright and Richard L. Watson, p. 312-328. Washington, D.C.: 31st Yearbook of the National Council for the Social Studies, 1961.

*"Change and New Perspectives." *American Studies in Transition*, edited by Marshall W. Fishwick, p. 101-113. Philadelphia: University of Pennsylvania Press, 1964. (Reprinted, Boston: Houghton-Mifflin, 1969.)

"The Etchings of Frederick Robbins," *New Hampshire Profiles* 20 (December 1969): 26-29.

"Vernon Louis Parrington." In *Pastmasters, Some Essays on American Historians*, edited by Marcus Cunliffe and Robin Winks, p. 142-166. New York: Harper & Row, 1969.

(With Leonard C. Wood.) *America, Its People and Values*. New York: Harcourt Brace Jovanovich, 1971. 848p.

"Reader's Encyclopedia of the American West," scheduled for publication in 1974 by Crowell of New York, will contain entries by this author on: Religious Sects and the West; Revivals and Revivalism; History of the Five Civilized Tribes (Cherokee, Choctow, Creek, Chickasaw, and Seminole).

"Wilbur Lucius Cross" entry for the *Dictionary of American Biography*. New York: Scribner's, Supplement Four scheduled for publication in 1974-1975.

Index

Abbot, Lyman, 139
Abolition movement, 130-1
Adams, Henry, 107
Agriculture, Department of, 191
Almagordo Air Base, 82, 87
American Communist party, 163
American Council of Learned
  Societies, 109
American democratic faith, ix,
  xvii, xviii, 3-15, 21-2, 27-31,
  34-8, 52, 66, 95, 106, 115-6,
  131-2
American Fellowship of
  Reconciliation, 74
American mythology. *See*
  Mythology
American Sociological Review, xi
American Studies, xvi; at Yale,
  xvii; at American University,
  xxi
American Studies Association, xxi
American University, xxi
Anglicans, statement of fourteen,
  122, 143
Anthropology, xii, 21; and
  cultural relativity, 150
Anti-intellectualism, 48, 143

Appeal to Reason (Paine), 52
Archbishop of Canterbury, 122
Architecture in America, 200,
  201, 202, 203
Ark, 120
Arms race, 86-7, 99-100
Arnold, Thurman, 74
Art: in Western civilization,
  153-4; museums, 179; in
  American life, 200-4; values in,
  203-4
Art Institute, Chicago, 202
Articles of Confederation, 44, 160
Asia, contributions to American
  civilization, 200
Atomic bomb, x, 82, 85-7; failure
  of disarmament negotiations,
  89; and nationalism, 91, 97, 145
Atomic Commission of United
  Nations, 85
Atomic Energy Commission, 89

Bach, Johann Sebastian, 19
Bacon, Leonard, 13
Balance of terror. *See* Churchill,
  Winston, 86
Ballot, secret, 162

219